ROSES

FOR

ENJOYMENT

There are many books on roses but here is one that is refreshingly different and eminently practical. So many writers regard exhibiting as the
ultimate aim of all rose growers. Gordon Edwards grows roses for enjoyment. He chose them because he regarded them as the most labour-saving
as well as the loveliest of flowers and now in his Sussex garden he has
over two thousand bushes which he tends himself mainly at week-ends.
He has been an outstandingly successful grower and in this book he sets
out to show how he has achieved his own results with the minimum of
fuss and worry.

His style is light but never superficial. Step by step he instructs his
readers in the whole art of rose growing but he does it in such an original
and entertaining manner that one highly experienced rose grower de-
clared, after reading the manuscript, that it was the only book on rose
growing he had been able to read and enjoy from end to end.

Mr Edwards' recommendations as to culture are entirely based on what
he has himself found successful and his comments on varieties are equally
personal. Every rose he describes, recommends or condemns he has tried
in his own garden. Every picture in this book, and there are plenty of them,
was taken in Mr Edwards' garden. They add enormously to its usefulness.

The colour plates of roses equally show what the roses depicted may be
expected to produce under ordinary garden conditions. They are not
pampered show blooms picked out from scores of rejects but typical
blooms grown by Mr Edwards for garden display.

Another unique feature of this book is its section on the rose grower's
budget. Mr Edwards is a methodical gardener and he likes to know what
things cost. He has come to the conclusion that his own roses for capital
and maintenance cost him less than one shilling apiece per annum. This,
he thinks, is resoundingly good value for money.

There is no good reason why any reader of his book should not enjoy
equally gratifying results.

ROSES
for Enjoyment

GORDON EDWARDS

LONDON

W. H. & L. COLLINGRIDGE LTD

First published in 1962
by W. H. & L. Collingridge Ltd
2–10 *Tavistock Street, London W.C.*2
Printed in Great Britain by
Balding and Mansell Ltd
London & Wisbech

Contents

PART FIVE: HOW THEY ARE LOOKED AFTER

PART SIX: HOW MUCH THEY COST

Illustrations

'If this man only understood the growing
of roses, he would be the most completely
perfect character on the face of creation!'

SERGEANT CUFF
The Moonstone

Alas! like man, no rose is perfect.

ACKNOWLEDGEMENT

IT was said of the present writer in his early manhood that if he had a
problem, the whole world had a problem: we do not change. This is
the reason why space does not allow me to name all those to whom a
debt is owed. Nevertheless, I must express my gratitude for all that I
have learnt over the years about roses from the publications of the
National Rose Society and to the contributors thereto. I am also most
grateful to my friends in the rose trade for so readily responding to
my requests for information.

As to the book itself: I offer to Peter Ayres my thanks for his
patience and my tribute to his skill in doing the photography for all
the plates in the open air of my garden (with one obvious exception).

The Library of the Royal Horticultural Society was, as always, its
efficient and most courteous self.

In lighter vein, I acknowledge my indebtedness to the late Mr
Wilkie Collins for making available, through the medium of *The
Moonstone*, the views on roses of Sergeant Cuff — thereby leaving only
the bees to that detective's illustrious successor — Sherlock Holmes.

Cuckfield,   GORDON EDWARDS
Sussex, 1962

Introduction

THE imprint on this book is 1962. Had it been 1862 the title would undoubtedly have been 'Roses Explained' or 'Understand your Roses'. Indeed, more certainly the two alternatives would have been combined. The book does, in fact, try to give information and explanations. Not, however, in the Victorian spirit of uplift, but in the belief that the enjoyment of any subject can be enhanced immeasurably by knowing something about it. From my own experience this is very true of roses.

Most of us buy our roses — nearly twenty-five million of them each year — from those enticing catalogues, so this book is in large part about their contents. But first of all there is some information as to how the roses get into the catalogue. Afterwards there is quite a bit about how they might best be used and treated so as to get the greatest pleasure from them.

Something had better be said about credentials, or the lack of them. Long hours of work following the war made me try to reduce to a minimum the upkeep of even a small garden. The replacement of a herbaceous border by fifty rose bushes was an obvious beginning. Now, nearly fourteen years later, there are, I suppose, some two thousand roses of all kinds, in a very much bigger garden. This book is, however, for the gardener who has in mind anything from a couple of dozen to a couple of hundred or so roses of various kinds — it is certainly not for the gardening tycoons. Throughout I have been a strictly week-end gardener. Perforce, therefore, and perhaps a little by inclination I am among those of whom William Paul wrote in 1848 — 'every one who cultivates roses may not do so with the design of becoming a candidate for floricultural honours; many are satisfied with the calm enjoyment which this, in common with other branches of Gardening, affords — the quiet mind, the healthful glow, yields them a sufficient recompense, and ample satisfaction'.

I have no greenhouse so there is nothing about growing roses in that way. I have done no original research into the history of the rose, so nothing can be said under that head. All the varieties mentioned in the book are growing in my garden or were grown in the old one.

The varieties illustrated were photographed in my garden in the varying conditions in which we see our roses. Some, for example Plates 15 and 18, were photographed in early June 1961, while others such as Plates 39 and 40 were taken late in September of that year (when incidentally the colour tones of many varieties are deeper). Seven plates (16, 41, 43, and 67 to 70) were taken immediately after six hours of steady rain. It also will be noticed that the blooms illustrated are in various stages of development: for example, while those in Plate 19 may be at their best there is also much to admire in the full blown beauty of the flowers in Plate 38. Unlike my childhood the visit of the photographer was not preceded by special dressing nor were the petals, like my hair, the subject of attention from exceedingly hot curling irons. In most of the groups one variety is on its own bush — in Plate 15 for example this is Michèle Meilland.

I am, I hope, no purblind specialist, but, like Sergeant Cuff, 'when I have a moment's fondness to bestow, most times, the roses get it'.

So pray read on, remembering what those fifty rose bushes have grown to. You have been warned. But perhaps in childhood you collected foreign stamps or the like. I never did.

By the way, rose growing, like medicine, is not an exact science.

PART ONE

How they are made

Plant Production and Reproduction
Producing and testing New Varieties
The Rose Nurseryman and his Year

I

Plant Production and Reproduction

A PACKET of seed for Tender and True parsnips, but an actual Home Guard potato for more Home Guard potatoes. An acorn for an oak tree, but a graft for an apple tree. Why the difference?

The whole aim and object of a plant's life is to reproduce itself, and broadly speaking most plants contain within themselves the power of reproduction, which as with most living things is the fertilization of female cells or eggs by male seed or pollen.

In flowers this pollen is produced and carried on the stamens, while the embryo seeds, or ovules as they are called, are embedded in the receptacle — the green case on which the petals are fixed — at the top of which is the stigma. When pollen is brought into contact with the stigma the ovules are fertilized. In due course, the flower dies off, the receptacle ripens into a seed container which may be an actual pod like the pea pod, a fruit like the apple, or a hep on the rose (Plates 12 and 100). Later on the seeds are released and dispersed and grow into new plants.

Most flowers are reproduced by themselves; that is to say, the ovules are fertilized from the flower's own pollen. Their offspring will have the same general shape and characteristics of their kind. But pollen is blown about by the wind and carried around in the peregrinations of insects — notably the bee — so that it may alight on the stigma of quite a different kind of plant. But unless the two plants are of the same species or of two closely related species no fertilization will take place; thus the pollen from a dandelion can fall like rain on the stigma of a daisy, but no seed will be produced. On the other hand the pollen, for instance, of one kind of wild, that is, a species rose, will fertilize the ovules of another kind. The result of this cross-fertilization among plant species is called a hybrid.

What kind of plants will the seeds of this crossing produce? Some will tend to be very like the plant which supplied the pollen and some will be similar to the plant which had its ovules fertilized. Others, however, will have some of the characteristics of each. This process of cross-fertilization can continue among the hybrids and results in more and more variation in the offspring, so that if one wants to reproduce a particular hybrid it certainly will not be achieved by saving its seed. In fact the only way to do it is by taking a piece of the plant and either getting it to root itself or to provide it with some other roots.

Earlier it was said that the offspring of a self-fertilized plant will be a reproduction of the parent plant. In general this is true, but small variations may occur in the offspring from time to time. The process, called natural selection — in effect the survival of the fittest — encourages useful variations (e.g. increased vigour) and may allow harmless ones (e.g. brighter colour) to persist. These variations breed true to type, and so new varieties appear.

Nature, however, has not been left to go her own way unassisted. Man over the ages has taken a hand in both processes and indeed has combined them. He has hurried along the selective process by crossing artificially within a particular species plants showing some enhanced characteristic compared with their fellows, e.g. greater fragrance, more robust growth, greater seed production, or more intense colour. He has continued this selection from generation to generation until he has in effect evolved quite different and far superior varieties.

Then he has cross-pollinated artificially the species with the varieties he has evolved, interbred their offspring with themselves and their parents and so produced still more varieties.

We can now answer from this highly simplified explanation the question opening this chapter. The way a variety of plant has been produced decides how it is going to be reproduced.

Thus the packet of parsnip seeds will produce Tender and True parsnips — certainly true, but the tender part will depend on how well they are grown and cooked. But sow the seed from the flowers of Home Guard potatoes, what then? A very mixed bag of potatoes would result: some like the immediate parents; some like the grandparents and so on through the other ancestors. How then do we get a crop of Home Guard potatoes? Simply by using the 'buds' of the potatoes and not the seed. The buds are, of course, the 'eyes' which we are enjoined to 'sprout' before planting, and when short of 'seed' potatoes we make them go further by cutting the potato up so as to give an eye to each piece.

Similarly the oak tree, having evolved, can be reproduced from its own acorns, while the seeds from, say, a Cox's Orange Pippin, the result of hybridization, will behave like those of the Home Guard potato. In short, varieties of plants produced by hybridization can only be reproduced from a piece of themselves, that is, what is termed vegetatively. This piece may be, for example, the eye of a potato, a cutting from a shrub, or a graft from an apple tree.

This is the position with our roses. They are an outstanding example of the results of hybridization. The R.H.S. Dictionary of Gardening says 'no group of plants in cultivation is of such mixed parentage as the roses seen in our British gardens and few decorative plants can have so long a horticultural history'. This being so they have to be reproduced either by a form of grafting, known as 'budding', on to a root stock, or by cuttings. The latter method, however, for the reasons given in Chapter III, is not favoured. The complex make-up also makes it a much harder task for the rose hybridist to produce a satisfactory new variety.

It is a common feature of vegetative reproduction that gradually the strain weakens. I suppose there may be, on a rough guess, some thirty million plants in existence of the variety Peace: it is a staggering thought that all of them have come from one small seedling plant, raised in the South of France in 1942, which came from one seed and probably yielded no more than three or four budding eyes. There is no sign of Peace deteriorating. Other factors are involved, but it is reasonably clear that the less complex the make-up of a variety and the nearer it is to the species roses the greater the likelihood of vigour and long life. It is of interest in this connection that of about 125 true species roses only some 12 have so far been used successfully in hybridization. The species rose, *Rosa foetida bicolor*, appears in the later ancestors of Peace and its presence suggests that Peace will continue for many generations. On the other hand, of the 120 hybrid tea varieties in the average rose catalogue today only about 30 appeared in the lists of 1938 and of these only three or four go back as far as 1913.

A tail-piece must be added: sometimes a plant of a variety will 'sport', that is, it suddenly produces a new characteristic, either wholly or in part. For example, a particular stem may bear flowers of quite a different colour to those of the rest of the plant or, as is not uncommon among roses, a bush may throw up long shoots and so become a climber. If the new characteristic is 'fixed', as it can be by budding, then the sport becomes a new variety in its own right.

B

II

Producing and testing New Varieties

LET us see what the modern rose hybridist has to do to get a new variety which is worthy to compete with those already available or to take the place of those which have deteriorated.

Hybridizing like other activities has its amateurs as well as its professionals. And very well the amateurs have done us too. But while they can and do keep up with professionals in quality they hardly match them in quantity. Nevertheless, they have to go through the same processes and operations even though they may handle fewer seedlings. I am, however, going to describe the activities of a large-scale hybridist who is out to produce at least one new variety each year—he may, of course, get more.

His first requirement is a very real love of roses. Then he will need quite a large area of glasshouses in which one will be the actual hybridizing house (in warmer climates hybridizing can be done in the open); this house must be quite insect-proof. Along the whole length, divided by a central gangway, will run two beds at about ground level. In these beds are planted some 300 seed parents. As already indicated the selection of these and the pollen parent calls for great skill — a skill which needs many years of experience to acquire and must constantly be adjusted and replenished. His selection will depend on knowledge of the parents' characteristics — good and bad — those of their ancestors (and there are so many) and, most important, the qualities he wants to see in the new hybrids.

These seed parents, protected as they are by glass, will usually be larger and more prolific of bloom than when you and I grow the same varieties outside. And well they might be, because the hybridist will make, between April and July, anything up to 15,000 crossings with the pollen from varieties growing either under glass or in the rose fields. Both skill and timing are necessary. The pollen must be ripe and ready, the temperature just so and, of course, the female parent must be prepared for the reception of the pollen on its stigma. This is done by the removal of the anthers before the pollen can get on to the stigma. Each crossing must be labelled and recorded.

Thereafter two hours every day of the week will be taken up in hoeing the beds, removing dead seed pods, inspecting for disease, spraying and in general maintenance. In addition the old petals must be removed continuously from the seed pods (heps) to facilitate their ripening and to prevent them rotting from accumulated moisture.

The ripening seed pods can be quite beautiful in themselves, but the hybridist would be less than human if he did not ignore their beauty and speculate about what the seed will produce: perhaps another Peace? By October the pods have been picked, but they will continue to be ripened, usually in damp vermiculite at a temperature of 60°F. The seeds — from three to twenty in each pod — will be sown in the seedling houses about Christmas time. Not all of them will germinate and others will be very slow in so doing, but the examination and tending of those that do will keep hybridist and staff busy. Flowers may be expected on the seedlings some three and a half months after sowing, i.e., in the following April. Naturally not all the seedlings will flower at the same time and during the flowering period of about ten weeks they will have to be examined twice a day to spot the likely winners. Seedlings and their first flowers are much smaller than the garden rose so that judgement of their potential is not easy. Moreover, flowering, foliage and general performance under glass are no final criterion of performance outside. But judge them the hybridist must, unless he is prepared to put up to 150,000 seedlings into his fields.

Among the hybrid tea seedlings there will be many 'singles' (see page 43 and Plates 72 and 97) and no skill is necessary to throw them out. Some seedlings will, however, test the hybridist's experience and he may wish to see a second flowering before deciding whether they warrant further consideration. For one reason or another he will reduce the 150,000 to something less than 4,000. Buds from these will be put on to under stocks out in the open in July and August.

During the following year he will be judging them again and he will probably decide that out of the 4,000 some 150 are worth keeping an eye on, and he will bud up more stocks of each — 25 or 100 according to judgement. Another summer will come and again judgement will be passed. A promising hybrid tea will go out because of insufficiency of petals, another seems a martyr to disease, in another the petals are soft so that the bloom does not open in a damp atmosphere, i.e., it 'balls' (Plate 1). A floribunda seedling shows a wonderful truss of flowers, but on closer examination there is little or no foliage. Another gives a first class truss and excellent foliage, but never a sign of new growth. Then there will be a rose that seems pretty good all round, but has to be eliminated because the petals of the dead flowers stick on like glue. Others go out because they are too much akin to existing varieties. This judging must be done daily, up and down the rows. The hybridist will not only be eliminating but also noting carefully the characteristics of the seedlings from the same parents as a guide to future crossings. At the end of each day he will have walked miles in a highly concentrated and exacting task.

The 150 seedlings will now be down to about 30 which he thinks worthy of serious consideration. Plants of these will be sent to the National Rose Society Trial Ground and to those in Europe, to fellow hybridists and to rose nurserymen likely to be interested. If, thereafter, he decides to put out a particular variety he will not be ready to do so before he has built up a sufficiency of stock. This sufficiency of stock is an all-important factor, because once he begins to sell he no longer controls his product, in that by grafting and budding his competitors can in the following year put as many plants of the new variety on the market as he can, or more. As an illustration of this it is said that in two months 50,000 budding eyes were obtained from 25 plants of the variety Queen Elizabeth. This may be something of an exaggeration, but there is no reason to think that it is a gross one. Be this as it may, the hybridist will find that before he begins to sell his new variety six to eight years will have elapsed since that sunny day when he put the pollen of Pretty Polly onto the stigma of Maid Marjorie.

Who are the people who give us these new roses? Here are the names of some of them together with examples of their most successful varieties in this country — old and new.

IN THE BRITISH ISLES

Herbert Robinson: *Christopher Stone, Gay Crusader, Mary Wheatcroft, Dorothy Peach, Westminster, Highlight.*

E. B. Le Grice: *Dainty Maid, Dusty Maiden, Ellinor Le Grice, Allgold, My Choice.*

Alex. Dickson: *Betty Uprichard, Shot Silk, Margaret, Shepherd's Delight, Silver Lining, Dearest.*

1. (Left) 'Balling' — blooms failing to open owing to rain or heavy dews. 2. (Right) Eden Rose planted April 1959, on canina stock; over 6 ft. high and very vigorous. 3. (Below) The same variety in similar soil and with identical treatment on laxa stock; vigorous but only 4 ft. high.

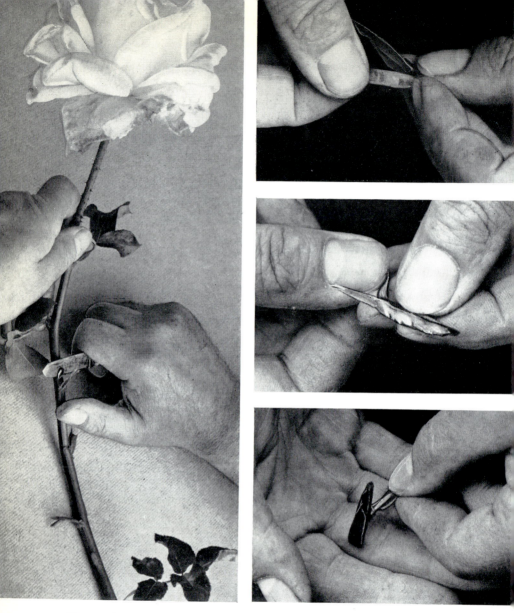

Budding: 4. 'Budding eye' being cut from a stem (thorns having been removed) which has carried a good bloom. The best buds are usually those in the middle of the stem; 5. the bark having been pulled back from the wood just up to the bud, the wood is removed with a twisting motion; 6. wood removed and the leaf stalk reduced to $\frac{3}{4}$ in. to serve as a handle; 7. lower end of the shield trimmed to about $\frac{1}{2}$ in. and ready for insertion in the stock.

Samuel McGredy (family): *Cynthia Brooke, Hector Deane, Picture, McGredy's Yellow, Mrs Sam McGredy, Orangeade, Piccadilly.*

AMONG THE AMATEURS

A. Norman: *Frensham, Ena Harkness.*

Oliver Mee: *Ethel Sanday.*

Bertram Park: *June Park, Lady Zia.*

IN FRANCE

Jean Gaujard: *Opera, Rose Gaujard.*

Charles Mallerin (the late): *Mme Henri Guillot, Virgo, Beauté, Danse du Feu.*

F. Meilland (the late): *Peace, Eden Rose, Grand'mère Jenny, Tzigane, Michèle Meilland, Alain.*

IN GERMANY

Wilhelm Kordes: *Crimson Glory, Gail Borden, Perfecta, Orange Triumph, Korona, Iceberg, Frühlingsgold, Frühlingsmorgen.*

M. Tantau: *Konrad Adenauer, Super Star.*

IN HOLLAND

G. de Ruiter: *Salmon Perfection, Red Wonder, Rosemary Rose.*

IN DENMARK

Svend Poulsen: *Karen Poulsen, Else Poulsen, Poulsen's Bedder, Tivoli, Sundance, Rumba.*

IN THE UNITED STATES

H. Swim (Armstrong Nurseries): *Sutter's Gold, Helen Traubel, Circus, Mojave.*

E. S. Boerner (Jackson & Perkins): *Fashion, Firecracker, Vogue, Jiminy Cricket, Masquerade.*

Dr W. E. Lammerts: *Charlotte Armstrong, Chrysler Imperial, Show Girl, Queen Elizabeth.*

The rose may be England's national flower but it is certainly of great interest elsewhere.

Most of the hybridists named have had a life-time of experience, some indeed have succeeded fathers and grandfathers, but perhaps of particular interest is that a younger generation is already carrying on the good work. In this one thinks of the friendly rivalry growing up between Neils Poulsen, Reimer Kordes, Sam McGredy IV, Pat Dickson and Alain Meilland.

These then are some of the people who are producing our new roses. But what of the new varieties themselves? To parents all geese are swans and the rose hybridists are human too. It is greatly to their credit that they are very ready to put their rose offsprings to the test. It may, therefore, be convenient at this point to give some explanation of the rose trials already mentioned — especially so because the results are almost invariably referred to in the catalogues issued by the rose nurserymen.

TESTING OF NEW VARIETIES

NATIONAL ROSE SOCIETY

The rose hybridist who wants to have a new variety tested by the National Rose Society has to send six plants to the Trial Ground at St Albans, Hertfordshire. Here over a period of up to three years they will be observed by an expert committee of amateur and professional rose growers. If on its performance the committee consider that the variety should do reasonably well — proper cultivation being understood — in most gardens, then it awards a *Trial Ground Certificate.**

In making judgement the following qualities are taken into account:

Vigour of growth; habit of growth; freedom from disease; beauty of form and/or garden value; colour; freedom and continuity of flowering; fragrance and general effect.

The standard is high, very high. In the twelve years 1949–1960 some 2,300 new varieties were offered for trial, while in the corresponding period of years only 331 certificates were awarded. And it is of interest on more than one account — including the indication of the esteem in which the foreign breeder holds these trials — that nearly 1,400 (60 per cent) of the entry came from abroad and gained 70 per cent — 230 — of the certificates.

A new variety, having gained a Trial Ground Certificate, is eligible to be put forward for the award of the *Society's Gold Medal* or its *Certificate of Merit.* The Gold Medal is for varieties which, in addition to satisfying the conditions for the Certificate, 'have some novel or

* Referred to in some catalogues as a First Class Certificate, but as there is no 'Second Class', the 'First Class' has no significance at all. (This must not be confused with the award of the same name by the Royal Horticultural Society.)

outstanding quality or supersede a similar variety which has declined'. As may be inferred the Certificate of Merit is for the varieties which do not quite make the Gold Medal grade. These awards are made by a differently composed committee to that judging at the Trial Ground, but normally part of the membership is common to both. The varieties put forward are judged on the show bench as to:

Novelty; beauty of form or truss; colour; fragrance and general effect;

but in arriving at the final assessment the points gained at the Trial Ground are taken into account and at an enhanced value (a ratio of 3:2). During the twelve-year period already mentioned 65 varieties were judged to be worthy of the Gold Medal, that is, one in six of those gaining the Trial Ground Certificate. Of the 65 Gold Medals 60 per cent went to varieties raised abroad.

The Certificate of Merit went to a further 100 varieties, so that in total (165) one in two of the Trial Ground Certificate qualifiers were regarded as something better than 'doing reasonably well in most gardens'.

The National Rose Society makes two other awards. One is the *President's International Trophy for the Best New Seedling Rose of the Year*, and it goes to the new variety judged as showing itself to be 'the most outstanding at the Society's Trial Ground and on the show bench' — in short, the best of the Gold Medallists of that particular year, which may, of course, produce an outstandingly good lot or less so. Then there is the *Clay Challenge Vase* awarded each year for the best-scented new British rose among those gaining the Gold Medal or Certificate of Merit.

ROYAL HORTICULTURAL SOCIETY

The Royal Horticultural Society gives an *Award of Merit* 'to plants and flowers which show a sufficiently distinct advance on their predecessors'. New varieties of roses are frequently, but not invariably, offered for consideration. (The possession of a National Rose Society Trial Ground Certificate is not a preliminary condition and anyone owning a plant can put it forward.) In the twelve-year period quoted, 137 such awards were made to roses.

TESTS ABROAD

In the United States there is an organization conducted by the rose trade called the All-America Rose Selections under which new varieties are judged for a two-year period at trial grounds up and down the country, the final decision being taken centrally. The American Rose Society also makes awards. New roses are also tested and judged in one way or another in Paris (where the Bagatelle Contest of open air trials have been in existence for over fifty years), in Lyons, Rome, Madrid, Geneva, The Hague, and in Scandinavia. The results have one common and rather depressing feature: until 1959 no British-raised roses featured in the post-war awards since a lone success in 1947. We must hope that a success in 1959, followed by four in 1960, is an indication that something of our pre-war pre-eminence in this field is returning.

HOW NEW VARIETIES
BECOME AVAILABLE TO THE PUBLIC

Before leaving the production of new varieties it might be well to explain how the rose trade operates in making them available to the public. Judging by the questions one is asked and the comments made at rose shows it seems that many find the subject confusing.

The professional hybridist in this country is usually also a rose nurseryman, that is, he produces rose plants for sale. Naturally he will himself put his own new varieties on the market. It has already been mentioned that once a new variety is on the market here the hybridist or 'raiser', as he is usually called, loses control of it and of the price in which he will have included a premium to help him to recoup his hybridizing costs (a new variety is usually 10s. 6d. compared with the standard price of 5s.). He may, therefore, make arrangements with other nurserymen to carry his new variety from the beginning and in return he will receive from them part of the premium. The function of these other nurserymen is that of distributors.

The hybridist abroad, and the amateur, will have no sales organiza-tion in this country, so arrangements will be made with a nurseryman here to introduce their new varieties. Since some 70 per cent of the new varieties put out in this country come from abroad these 'new introductions' are a prominent feature. Nevertheless there is an important distinction between a rose having been 'raised' and having been 'introduced'. Just to make things a little more difficult, it must be added that a hybridizing nurseryman may also act as an introducer. He is not likely, however, to leave his customers in any doubt as to which is which!

III

The Rose Nurseryman and his Year

OUR prime interest as gardeners will be with the ordinary run of varieties which we buy to the tune of nearly 25 million a year. These are produced by many thousands of nurserymen ranging from the small (and so useful) local man round the corner, who produces a few thousand rose plants among his other stock, to the giants of the rose trade who think in terms of hundreds of thousands. Whatever the quantity produced the operations involved in making a rose plant, whether it be bush, standard, shrub or climber, are essentially the same, and I think they will be of interest.

In the dark of a November evening in 1960 I was visiting a rose nurseryman and looking at his new packing and dispatch arrangements; these, incidentally, were so good that despite the appalling weather conditions at that time they had enabled him to get away a higher number of orders than in the corresponding period in earlier years. Going from one shed to another I stumbled over several huge straw bundles — like those in which we receive our roses, only some ten times as big. The contents? About 400,000 rose stocks, to be unpacked, planted out, budded and then harvested like any other crop. The nurseryman's year had not yet finished but another had already begun. Actually it had begun some time before the arrival of those bundles because the ground had had to be ploughed, harrowed, fertilized and so on. Again like other crops, the same land will not be used year after year for rose production. A strict crop rotation is not necessarily used, but having carried a crop of roses a piece of land will ordinarily be rested for at least two years. During that time it may lay fallow, be used to run sheep or cattle, or to grow a crop of grass or oats (which explains where some of that packing straw comes from).

Before going further with the grower's cycle of operations to produce our roses something should be said about propagation and rose stocks.

CUTTINGS

Many gardeners will know that there is nothing easier than to increase one's bushes of blackcurrants, gooseberries, and many shrubs by taking cuttings, indeed that is precisely how many of them are produced commercially. One's stock of roses can also be increased in this way, but commercially it just is not worthwhile because the proportion which root is extremely low and when rooting does take place such a long period of growth is necessary to obtain a worthwhile plant. We gardeners would certainly fight shy of the price which would of necessity have to be demanded. The only possible exception to this general statement is, as will appear later, some of the very vigorous climbers. This does not mean that amateur gardeners (to whom time should matter less) should not have a shot at propagating roses from cuttings. They may, however, like first to consider my own experience, which, without going into too much detail, shows that in 1951, full of the idea of making cheap roses, I put out in the early autumn some 330 cuttings. They were taken from the growth of that year, about 10 in. long, and pencil thick, cut just below a budding eye (see page 28), all the leaves removed except a few at the top, treated with the appropriate grade of hormone root-forming powder, planted and firmed in about 6 in. deep and 6 in. apart. The soil was well drained and sandy. I was prepared to leave them there until the following November twelvemonth. Of the 330 cuttings, 42 had rooted by the spring of 1952; of these during the next few years 16 faded away or were not worth keeping. The remaining 26 were made up of 21 climbers; The New Dawn (2 strikes out of 4 cuttings), Albertine (16 out of 17), Sander's White (3 out of 6), and the floribunda Frensham (5 out of 30). All the other floribundas and all the hybrid teas were unsuccessful.

Dr R. Selby describes in articles in *The Rose* (Spring 1956 and Spring 1961), a much more extensive operation — involving some 1,600 cuttings of all kinds. Coincidentally the percentage rooting was practically the same as my own experience — 13 per cent. Dr Selby, however, has watched his 207 over ten years and recorded their fate. In the result only 89 survive, the remaining 118 having died or having been discarded as not worth retention. Out of 1,600 cuttings, therefore, 5 per cent ultimately survived. As Dr Selby points out it is the climbers and ramblers which do well, and a higher rooting rate may be expected the nearer the variety is to the wild (species) rose: in short, he says, the results of much labour satisfied curiosity, but little else.

But by all means try propagating from cuttings. You may get a successful 'take' and, like winning a raffle, you will be pleased out of all proportion. Such propagation is obviously not a commercial proposition and the private gardener's time, save in the field of the ramblers, can be much more profitably spent. By the way, there is a very old piece of gardening folk-lore that rooting is much encouraged by splitting the end of the cutting up an inch and inserting a grain of wheat. I have not tested it, but anyway, how many gardeners have grains of wheat around?

ROSE STOCKS

Roses then are raised not on their own roots but on stocks from the species and their near relatives. Very few such stocks are produced here; practically all are imported — in 1960 nearly thirty-four million — from Holland (mainly), Denmark, Belgium and West Germany. There are many varieties of stocks and some are produced from both cuttings and seeds. The most commonly used in this country is canina, of which there are many variations. Canina stocks are said to produce the hardiest bushes, which transplant well and to be generally better suited to the soil of this country — maybe, but there are tremendous variations in the soil of this country. Laxa and multiflora stocks are also much favoured. The former is said to allow earlier and easier budding — it is practically thornless. Multiflora is specially recommended for lighter soils, but it is held not to do well on heavy ones. It is also said that the bushes grown on it have a shorter life than that given by canina stock. I have not, so far, found either criticism justified.

It may well be, however, that certain varieties do better on one kind of stock than on another. The plantings of Eden Rose in Plates 2 and 3 are of the same age, in the same kind of soil (only 6 ft. apart) and have been subjected to the same kind of pruning and culture. The one in Plate 3 is up to 4 ft. high and is on laxa stock; the other, Plate 2, is on a variety of canina and is up to 6 ft. high. Moreover, it is obviously more vigorous.

Rugosa is the stock now mainly used for standard roses: principally, I understand, because the country worker no longer has to add to his income by grubbing out suitable dog-rose (canina) stems from the copses and hedges.

I am not adding any more names of varieties of stocks because there are so many — as many as there are opinions among the rose nurserymen as to what is the best stock for them and for the customer.

Over a hundred years ago Sergeant Cuff gave his views with great firmness when he said 'And mind, if you ever take to growing roses, the white moss rose is all the better for *not* being budded on the dog-rose'. But he was equally firmly countered by the Scottish gardener whose opinion was 'The de'il a bit ye'll get the white moss rose to grow, unless ye bud him on the dogne-rose first'. Research is being done, and one day there may be rose stocks comparable in uniformity and standard as the various types of Malling stocks for apples. In the meantime we do not seem to be faring too badly. But if an amateur gardener finds that, despite good soil conditions and cultivation, his roses are doing less well than can be expected, he can certainly ask his supplier what stock is being used and then try one who buds on to a different kind. But I really do not think that the need to do this will arise in all but a very few cases.

Whatever stocks he favours the rose nurseryman will plan to get them planted during February to April as soil conditions allow. In the rows they will be about 9 in. apart and there will be 3 ft. between the rows. Those interested in figures may like to be reminded that this adds up to about 20,000 per acre. During the spring and early summer the stocks will have to be kept clean from weeds by hand, by mechanical hoeing or indeed by the plodding and instinctively careful horse-powered hoeing. In some areas spraying against early attacks of mildew may be necessary before early July when the all-important 'budding' season begins.

BUDDING

Budding, it has been mentioned, is a variety of grafting. It is illustrated in Plates 4 to 11, where the budding of a standard rose is shown. I believe this to be easier than bush stock on which to make one's first attempt at budding. The operation is essentially the same whether done for bush, climber or standard.

As Plate 4 shows the 'bud' is the embryo stem waiting to grow between a leaf stalk and the stem it springs from. The actual operation consists in cutting out buds, in shield shape, from a stem which has borne a good quality flower — the best buds are usually in the middle of the stem — removing the wood by a quick corkscrew motion so as to leave the back of the bud undamaged; cutting the leaf stalk off, but leaving $\frac{3}{4}$ in. as a handle. A T-shaped cut is then made in the stock and the bark lifted so as to allow the bud to be inserted. The surplus at the

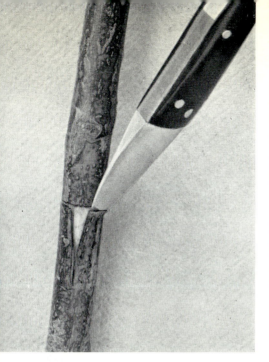
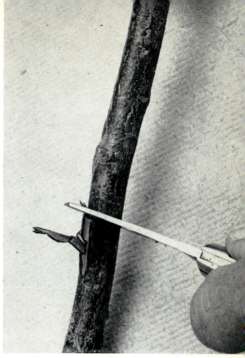

Budding: 8. 'T' cut made in bark of stock and the vertical edges raised to facilitate insertion of bud; 9. bud inserted and top end trimmed off level with horizontal cut; 10. binding up with damp raffia; 11. binding completed (if bud still green after about 14 days the operation has been successful). See also Plate 14.

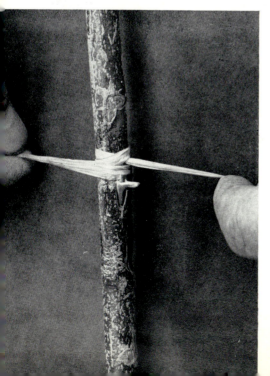
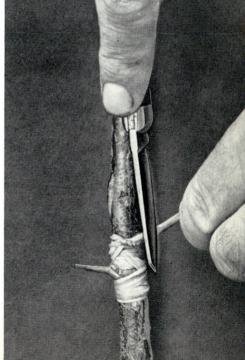

12. *An 8 ft. standard — the result of budding at 5 ft. instead of normal 3 ft. 6 in. (see the standard in background).*

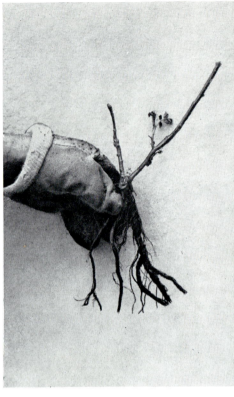

13. (Above) *A cheap maiden rose bush — two miserable stems; roots not too bad.*

14. (Left) *A quality maiden bush — four good stems and a good root system too. (Note the snag on left-hand side which was left to protect the bud when natural growth of the rootstock was cut back.)*

top of the shield is then trimmed off; the bark pushed back and then bound up with moistened raffia (in these days, however, plastic ties of various kinds are increasingly used). When budding bush stocks an essential preliminary is to scrape away the soil and to wipe clean the neck of the stock — after all, a surgical operation is involved. Those who want to begin their budding experience on bushes may prefer to use canina stocks grown from cuttings rather than from seed as they provide a larger area on which to operate.

Only one bud is used to produce a bush or climbing rose, but for standards usually three are inserted in the stock. In the case of rugosa stocks they are put into the main stem, but on canina stocks they each go into lateral shoots coming out of the main stem. (The stock used in the Plates is a variety of canina which is an exception to this rule.)

Although I am sure the warning is unnecessary I record my stupidity in my first essay in budding. I purchased twelve rugosa standard stocks, and although I was well aware that the accepted height for budding was 3 ft. 6 in., foreseeing failure, I left myself plenty of room for a second shot by inserting the buds at about 5 ft.

One knows about failure in under three weeks: if the bud has turned brown and shrivelled, one has had it. With beginner's luck I had eleven takes and those 'tree roses' remain to this day as monuments of a lapse from common sense. I should, of course, have budded at the customary height and worked up! However, I have since discovered that these super standards are popular on the continent, but they are better produced from a vigorous variety of floribunda rather than from a hybrid tea. Plate 12 shows one of these standards, which is 8 ft. high compared with the more normal 6 ft. of the one in the background.

The horticultural press usually contains names of suppliers of small quantities of rose stocks and budding wood. The rose you first successfully bud will be for ever after — to mix the metaphor — the apple of your eye. You are more likely to succeed if you avoid actual wet weather and if the work is done when the sap is flowing well: in very dry conditions it will not be so flowing, so give the stock a good soaking two or three hours before beginning operations. The professional budder with thousands of buddings to make cannot be quite so choosy about conditions. He will, however, need skill, speed, stamina and, if there be such a thing, green fingers. His operations are confined to the actual budding: the tying in with raffia or other kind of tie is done by a helper.

A budder is expected to do at least a thousand buds a day; most can do better than that and some very much better, say two thousand. Bonuses are often offered, usually for rates above 1,300. But a budding is useless unless it is successful, so any bonus systems usually take the percentage of success into account. A budder notching up a take of 85 per cent would be regarded as highly successful.

The successful 'takes' normally lie dormant until the following spring, but if exceptionally one gets away immediately it must be cut back to two 'eyes' and this means walking the rose fields to detect them. The percentage of successful takes can vary not only on account of the skill of the budder, but also from the general weather conditions of the particular year, the kind and quality of the stock in relation to the land and, as already noted, in relation to the particular varieties. While, since the very buds themselves vary in quality, there will be variation of quality in the successful takes. The rose nurseryman then, like the farmer, will talk of a good or not so good crop. It is these factors that account for the difference between the number of imported rose stocks and the number of plants sold.

By February in the following year the pressure of the growing union between bud and stock, combined with the weather, will rot and break the raffia ties, while the plastic ones will expand and eventually drop off. (The amateur will be able to inspect his ties and if any remain they should be removed.) The significance of February is that during this month the professional and amateur growers alike will have to cut off the growing top of the stocks. When doing this about 1 in. of stem of the stock above the bud will be left for its protection. This 'snag' is shown on the left-hand side of the plant illustrated in Plate 14.

We are now into year two in the production of the rose crop. During the warm spring days the buds will get away, not, fortunately, one shoot per bud; as mentioned on page 152, frost and other conditions, including natural vigour, will usually produce two, three or four, so that there are the beginnings of a nice plant. Where, however, multiple shoots are not produced naturally the nurseryman must walk the rows and pinch back the single shoots to induce more breaks from the bud.

Spraying against pests and diseases may be necessary and the crop will have to be kept clean. In June and July will come the blooms and a new plant has arrived. These new rose bushes have the charming name of 'maidens'. They will still need the attention of spray and hoe.

REQUIREMENTS FOR A QUALITY ROSE PLANT

Come October the crop is ready for lifting against the orders which have been flowing in ever since the catalogues were issued, the rose shows up and down the country have been held, and advertisements are appearing in the press. So far the nurseryman has been dealing with his crop in the mass, but with the execution of orders there will be inspection of the individual plants and, being individuals, their quality may vary. For a quality rose costing 5s. and upwards the customer has the right to expect a good root system (and this is seldom absent) and *not less than* two good stems. This is what the quality nurseryman will send him. Anything below this standard will be regarded as a second, to be disposed of wholesale as such, or retailed by the grower at a much reduced price at the end of the season. Plate 13 shows a bush rose with two miserable stems which cost 3s.; Plate 14 a first-quality rose at 5s.

At this date, happy is the nurseryman who two years previously estimated the quality and quantity of his crop and the public demand so accurately that his rose fields are empty. But life is not like this: what happens to what remains? Are they kept over for a sale next year? Not so: all those not required for the production of next year's budwood go to the bonfire. The rose nurseryman sells only maiden plants.

PART TWO

How they are sold

c

IV

Rose Nurserymen's Catalogues

SOME people will go to a horticultural show and, with or without the attendant's assistance, make their orders for roses on what they see on the stands. Others will buy their roses at a chain store. Some, more fortunate, will visit a rose nursery in the summer and look, listen and learn for themselves before making an order. But for most of us, roses, like seeds and other stuff for the garden, must be bought from the nurserymen's catalogues. It is for this reason, in particular, that this book follows broadly the layout and contents of these often fascinating productions in the hope that buyers of roses may understand them better and may therefore get the most from them and hence from their roses.

There is little doubt that the rose is the most popular cultivated flower, and one of the reasons is, I imagine, its highly individual characteristics. (If these have any general tendency I should say it is in the direction of feminism, but I am not prepared to particularize.) This individuality is certainly reflected in the catalogues which the rose nurserymen put out. And may they never lose it: a dull uniformity would take much of the colour and enjoyment out of one aspect of our gardening activities.

There are two things the rose nurseryman wants to do: to sell his roses and to give satisfaction to his customers. But the customers live in different parts of the country, the soil in their gardens is not all the same, the weather conditions vary and, such is the individuality of the rose, a variety which will do superbly in one neighbourhood gives no satisfaction in another. The nurseryman can hardly be expected to know just what will suit the circumstances of the individual customer, so that there must be limitations on the information he gives on this account, and on account of space too. Moreover the individual nurseryman's personal assessments of a variety's qualities, performance and usefulness, must inevitably show some variations. Here as an illustration are the descriptions from catalogues selected at random, of a hybrid tea variety similarly chosen:

A 'bi-colour of vivid scarlet and rose; fragrant; good growth'.

B 'Vivid scarlet misty rose bi-colour. There is nothing like it for colour. Makes a good bedding rose of medium habit, approximately 2–3 ft.'

C 'A unique bi-colour. Rich scarlet petals with a silver reverse. Very popular for exhibition work.'

D 'Medium to tall. Rich red with silvery reverse, a massive bloom of good shape. Bush strong and vigorous, foliage glossy. A wonderful piece of colour, gorgeous for flower arrangements.'

E 'Velvety scarlet inside the petals, outside veiled with a silver sheen. A large full flower of superb formation and great substance, freely borne on strong stems. Vigorous, with plentiful glossy foliage, excellent for garden, cutting and exhibitions.'

F 'A magnificent rose of unusual and intriguing colour. Velvety scarlet with silvery reverse: blooms are long lasting and the growth is vigorous.'

G 'Petals red inside, lighter outside. Flowers of medium size, rather blunt nosed. Scarcely fragrant. Upright growth of average height (3 ft.). We know that some people go for this one, but cannot get very fond of it ourselves. May black-spot.'

H 'Striking bi-colour of exquisite form. Large blooms of velvety vivid scarlet inside the petals, contrasting with a misty rose reverse.'

J 'Vivid scarlet on the inside, the outside is shaded misty white, a unique effect. The full flowers are freely produced on a good tree.'

K 'A large shapely flower of unusual and intriguing colours. Carmine-crimson with silvery reverse. Somewhat shy but the flowers are long lasting and the growth is vigorous.'

Indeed, truth has many aspects, but the basic information is there.

In reading the descriptions, however, it is well to keep certain points in mind. What the descriptions do not say is often as important as what they do say. For instance, if in a particular catalogue some

15. *Some hybrid teas — from the top — Spek's Yellow, a prolific bloomer; a bud and bloom of Michèle Meilland; Ena Harkness and Margaret show the much admired classical shape and size.*

17. *Mme Louis Laperrière, taken on the bush, is another very fragrant red with well shaped blooms 'moderately large' compared with the 'large' of Ena Harkness (Plate 15).*

16. *The light pink Monique gives cup-shaped blooms of much fragrance. The fragrance of Josephine Bruce is pronounced too; in the bed its crimson-scarlet is deeper than in the Plate.*

varieties are described as 'disease-resistant' and others are not so described, then it is a fair inference that the latter are not resistant — or, at best, they are less so. Again expressions such as 'at its best in sunny weather' or 'good under glass' may imply that the varieties so described will not stand up very well to rain.

In this connection I am almost inclined to say to the beginner that if he sees a variety of hybrid tea in which the word 'exhibition' appears in the description, he should not buy it. This would, however, be quite unfair, because in these days so many varieties are good both for exhibition and for the garden. But while the purely exhibition rose will certainly have wonderful form it may not have resistance to weather and it will need protection from the rain if one is to see it at its best or, indeed, see it otherwise than as a soggy ball of vegetable matter. At best one cannot expect many blooms. There is nothing more satisfying than the production of a perfect exhibition bloom, but I do suggest that in the early days of one's rose growing it is best to avoid varieties in which the catalogue description mentions the word 'exhibition'; go instead for those which say nothing about the purpose of the rose or talk about 'bedding'. Later on try one or two purely exhibition types — they can be very thrilling.

'BEDDING' AND 'DECORATIVE' ROSES

All roses are grown in beds of one kind or another, but the hybrid teas are often described under a general heading in catalogues as 'Bedding Roses'. Sometimes in the descriptions of particular varieties the expression 'an ideal bedding rose' is used. I am bound to say that in the past I have often been far from clear whether this meant that the particular variety was sturdy, rather below average height and giving lots of bright colour, or whether the flowers were rather formless so that the variety was unsuitable for exhibition work — or indeed that both applied, as it does to certain varieties.

But since there are now so few purely exhibition roses in the catalogues the distinction seems no longer very much in point. The description of 'bedding' in relation to hybrid teas seems even less helpful now that the floribunda type of rose (see Chapter VI) has, in the past thirty years, become the 'bedding rose' *par excellence*. 'Bedding rose', however, still lingers on and it seems to be attached in particular to the hybrid teas which make up in colour what they lack in shape, in size of bush and bloom, and give freely of their flowers. The expression 'decorative rose' is also used. Surely all roses are decorative.

No authoritative definition of what is a decorative rose seems to exist, but it appears to apply to varieties which, while not up to exhibition standard in size, have flowers of a good shape and which come freely. Mojave, Serenade and Virgo (Plates 19 and 40) are typical 'decorative' roses. Be all this as it may, the important thing for the ordinary rose grower is that the descriptions 'bedding' and 'decorative' are green lights, in contrast to the amber of 'exhibition'.

'VIGOUR' AND 'HEIGHT'

It may have been noticed that only two of the variety descriptions quoted earlier say anything very precise about height. One could wish that more did so. But, as mentioned earlier, performance can vary according to conditions. For instance in my virgin soil practically all kinds of roses are a quarter to a third higher than normal. Moreover, the difference in height between recognized tall and short growers is quite considerable. Some descriptions equate 'vigour' with 'height'. The National Rose Society does so and by 'moderately vigorous' means in reference to a bush rose that it has a normal growth of about 2 ft. 6 in., while 'vigorous' and 'very vigorous' indicate a capacity for increased growth accordingly. With respect, a miniature rose of 9 in. can be vigorous and it seems better to keep this term and height separate, as indeed the Society does in defining, in relation to hybrid teas, 'tall growing' as approximately 3 ft. 6 in. or over and 'shorter growing' as 'approximately 2 ft.' and in relation to floribundas substituting 4 ft. for the 3 ft. 6 in. These heights are in mind in drawing up the descriptions in Chapters V and VI, 'average height' being regarded as 3 ft. following moderate pruning (see page 151).

FRAGRANCE

If the rose catalogues are somewhat unforthcoming and sometimes inconsistent in what they say about fragrance it is not, as so many of the older generation would have it, that the hybridist has 'bred out' the fragrance of the old roses. One can name at least thirty hybrid tea roses introduced in the last fifteen years which could compete successfully with the most 'fragrant glories' of the good old days, which by the way, produced in 1900 that scentless cold white wonder Frau Karl Druschki. (Still obtainable and still worth growing.) Indeed, there are few modern roses for which a claim to some fragrance is not made. But I suspect that with quite a number of people the vegetable smell of all plant growth ranks as 'slightly fragrant'.

The plain fact is that a sense of smell is a highly personal matter and one indeed which does not necessarily depend on the degree of one's smoking or snuffing, although in general the heavy smoker will not get the same degree of enjoyment from the fragrance of flowers as others do. Moreover, the time of day, humidity of the atmosphere, temperature (whether outdoor or indoors), winds and draughts can all affect the emission of scent from flowers, and the individual's detection and appreciation of it.

The compilers of some rose catalogues are brave enough to evaluate fragrance, often in three grades as 'some', 'strong', and 'very strong'. Do not condemn them if when you buy a variety its fragrance is not what you expected. Your 'some, strong and very strong' may be — 'none, a trace, and a bit'. Like the cheerfulness of my namesake Oliver Edwards, the friend of Dr Johnson, fragrance will creep in.

COLOUR ILLUSTRATIONS

There is no creeping in about those coloured illustrations in the catalogues. The variation in their quality is probably the most notable feature as between one catalogue and another. But even as regards the best (including those in this book) one must keep in mind the limitations of colour reproduction. Whites, yellows and the lighter pinks are almost invariably good, sometimes quite outstandingly so. But the reds, in all their variation, often leave much to be desired, while if the colour of the bloom seems to be right the green and bronzes of the foliage often look decidedly odd. Whether the colour work is 'bad, not too bad or good', our orders for roses are influenced by them. (Did the colour plates influence your purchase of this book?) A nurseryman who feels that a particular variety is neglected can do much to advance its sales by putting a colour picture in his catalogue.

There is nothing wrong about this aid to salesmanship and to the prospective buyer. It is mentioned here, however, in order that the influence the colour exerts may be kept in mind and to suggest that the reader of the catalogue should pay at least as much attention to the written description of the variety as to the colour reproduction. Another point to keep in mind is that the pictures are not invariably in the same scale in relation to each other nor, of course, to the actual roses.

USEFUL INFORMATION

Considering, however, the limitations imposed by the cost of production and by the cost of postage, a remarkable amount of useful information is given in many rose nurserymen's catalogues in addition to the descriptions of the varieties. For instance, of a sample of fourteen catalogues, nine of them not only tell one what to do with parcels of plants on arrival, but there is also extensive and very useful cultural information. The fact that five of the catalogues do not contain material of this kind does not necessarily mean that the firms were unhelpful or indifferent. Many rose nurserymen send most useful advice either when acknowledging one's order or when despatching it.

I will not add to this rather voluminous background except to note that expressions such as 'flowers come freely' are discussed in Chapter V.

TERMS OF BUSINESS

Let us now examine the catalogue of our choice or the one which came uninvited.

First, whether it be on the front page or the last, I suggest that one reads the 'Terms of Business'. A mundane topic perhaps, but an act of fairness to oneself and the nurseryman. It can be profitable to oneself as terms of carriage and the buying of quantities can vary. Orders above £5 are usually sent carriage free, while below that figure there is usually either a fixed charge or a sliding scale. Either way, if an order amounts to something below but near the carriage free level, another plant can often be added at little or no extra cost.

It is often worthwhile to pay attention to the rate offered 'per dozen'; not only because this usually gives twelve bushes for the price of eleven, but because that favourable rate frequently applies to a half dozen bushes of the same variety. Advice of this kind may seem pernickety and Scrooge-like, but gardeners have other responsibilities which give need to watch, if not the pennies, certainly the shillings. And anyway the nurseryman knows what he is doing when he offers the terms he does.

But what is a fair price to pay for one's roses? The price for the old-established varieties as compared with the new introductions is usually 5s. Of course one can buy cheaper than this: I have already mentioned the 'seconds' which the quality nurseryman will not dispose of himself or, if he does, it will be made quite clear what he is selling.

The horticultural and national press is, however, well supplied with advertisements offering roses in variety well below the standard price. My comment on this is to tell a story. I responded to such an advertisement in the winter of 1960 and ordered one dozen bushes of the hybrid tea variety Ann Letts at 2s. apiece, and one climbing Mme Butterfly at 3s. (normal price 6s. 6d.).

Properly treated 'seconds' and indeed the cheaper roses generally grow into good plants eventually. 'Eventually' is the key word as I have yet to see one which came up to a quality rose in the earlier years. There is, however, something else. Three of the Anne Letts were photographed for an article illustration and were left behind in the studio. The remaining nine flowered in due course and showed themselves to be one Anne Letts and eight floribundas of the variety called Circus. The climbing Mme Butterfly turned out to be a climbing Shot Silk which has yet to climb.

Unwearied in the search for a bargain I had another attempt in the spring of 1961 when in response to a newspaper advertisement I sent for half-a-dozen of a comparatively new floribunda at the very much cut price of 3s. each. I have yet to identify the variety I received, despite the fact that my order was marked 'no substitute'.

The plain fact is that one gets what one pays for, whether it be refrigerators or roses.

But to return to the 'Terms of Business'. They will usually contain a protection clause for the grower: it will normally guarantee 'all goods in his list to be healthy and true to name on leaving the nurseries' (there was, of course, no such guarantee in the advertisements I answered), but it will disclaim responsibility for what happens thereafter. That is perfectly fair, because what happens is beyond his control. Notwithstanding this, it has been my experience that where instructions issued by the nurseryman about planting and cultivation have been followed and he is satisfied on this point, favourable consideration is usually given to the replacement of failures. Some nurserymen give an unconditional guarantee. I have no experience of its operation.

NEW VARIETIES

Next in our catalogue is often something in a personal vein from the nurseryman. Do not pass it by. Some are stereotyped but most can tell quite a bit about the firm and reflect the personality of the writer — and those in the rose trade are very strong personalities. Here, where appropriate, will be announced the new varieties which are on offer for the first time.

One of the reasons for new varieties was explained in Chapter I but it is not the only one. It seems an inherent characteristic of man-

kind that it is attracted to the new: an attraction which often goes so
far as to believe implicitly that anything new is better than the old.
The rose lover well knows, or should do, that the perfect rose (like the
blue rose) has yet to come, but since hope springs eternal, there is
always the chance that this year's catalogue may contain it. So we are
quite ready with our half guineas — the standard price in the first
year.

Some people contend that there are too many new roses — there
were over thirty in 1960 and about the same number in 1961. But
they are answered by what I have said about the need for replacements and the fact that we gardeners are so very ready to buy them.
There are plenty of worse ways of spending one's money but roses
are not the only thing in the garden and one each of thirty varieties is
over £15.

However, the price of a new rose usually drops a shilling or so each
year until it is stabilized. If, then, we can bear to wait two or three
years there is a considerable saving. Waiting also has the advantage
that one can see how the variety has 'settled down'. Some new roses
seem to be splendid from the start; others take quite a time to get into
their stride or to reveal weaknesses. Recently there was a new rose
which performed marvellously as a maiden but which invariably col-
lapsed in its second or third year.

But how many of us can bear to wait? We can at least be selective
and try to assess the newcomers for ourselves when visiting shows and
nurseries. We can be keen to find out whether a variety has a National
Rose Society Trial Ground Certificate or better. We can keep in mind
that the most ballyhoo is not always for the best rose and *per contra* we
will not condemn a new rose simply because it attracts much publicity.

Beyond thoughts of this kind I cannot assist the inexperienced
except on one point — based firmly on my own experience, and
one you will find hard to adopt. It is that a fair and serious judgement
on a new variety is difficult to obtain from the experience of one plant
only, because the individual bushes vary. Three bushes of the variety
are more than three times more useful. I am probably wasting space
in saying it, but if you have three guineas to spend use it for two
varieties, not six.

With this background we can now study the various sections into
which the catalogues are divided.

V

Hybrid Teas

T HE Margaret and the Ena Harkness in Plate 15 are typical hybrid teas of classical shape and size. But how to define or describe the perfect hybrid tea? Dr J. H. Wilding of Bolton has answered this question in a standard of prose matching, if I may say so, that of his rose growing by saying — 'I can only gaze in wonder on the way the petals curl in several curves at once, each separate curve of each separate petal synchronizing in harmony with each other until they unite in the centre in a unified cone'. It is that high conical centre which many people find so attractive.

Plate 38, however, in Grand Gala, and Plate 16 in Monique, show a rather differently shaped bloom: it is cup-like or blunt-ended and rather like the shape of the old garden roses. Catalogues show a tendency to apply the description 'bedding', discussed earlier, to roses of this shape. Large blooms are by no means a *sine qua non* for beauty. The varieties giving much smaller and differently shaped blooms, such as Mojave and Spek's Yellow (Plates 40 and 15), are equally to be esteemed.

PETALS

The number, size and type of petal varies enormously among the varieties. There are *single*, that is, five-petalled, hybrid teas still catalogued, but it is among the other kinds that they are now mostly found (Dainty Maid, Plate 72 and Frühlingsmorgen, Plate 97). This also applies to *semi-double* blooms, which are those with not more than fifteen petals (Allgold, Plate 94). Above that number the description 'double or full' is applied. There are, however, degrees of fullness: thirty to forty petals would rank as *full* (Gail Borden, Plate 67), with *moderately full* (Virgo, Plate 19) and *very full* (Perfecta, Plate 38) for numbers below and above these figures.

As might be expected, varieties with the fewer petals — those in the

43

early twenties and below — tend to open very much more quickly
than the many-petalled ones. In the bud stage they can be just as
shapely, and they often make up for their fleetingness by coming
quickly in succession. Moreover, many people get pleasure from seeing
the centre of the rose with its stamens.

Short petals naturally do not produce a high centre but give the
cup-like shape mentioned earlier, but varieties so furnished invariably
have other qualities which appeal and make them well worth their
place in the rose beds.

An important feature of the petals — some would say the most
important — is their texture. Thin and papery usually means that
when wet they will stick together and the bloom will ball (see page
19). Unfortunately some very beautiful varieties, especially among
whites, creams and light pinks, have this fault which can be produced
by heavy falls of dew as well as by rain. The varieties in the catalogues
specially recommended for exhibition are often prone to this and
should be watched on this account.

The exhibitor will use shades to guard the blooms against the wet.
But as regards the ordinary grower I must say with great emphasis
that I know of nothing more disappointing in gardening than having
lavished care, time and attention on one's roses to find that in the end
the blooms are soggy balls like those in Plate 1. The wetness of
water does not vary in localities, although naturally some districts get
more rain than others. There is little excuse for putting out these days
a variety with this weakness, unless it is clearly indicated and there are
many countervailing qualities.

FREEDOM OF FLOWERING

The number of flower buds produced by the varieties is also subject
to variation. Some come one or two to each stem, others give three or
four, while a few give even more. In many varieties the second crop
especially gives whole chandeliers of buds — see Plate 101 — if fine
quality blooms are wanted then there must be much disbudding (see
page 171).

A variety's capacity for freedom of flowering or the reverse often
appears in catalogue descriptions, especially in the Hybrid Tea section,
and it may be helpful to say something about it. What is the standard of
'free'? Five blooms or fifty? Does it cover the blooms on the bush at
any particular time or over the whole flowering season? I take it to
mean the latter. And if one disbuds the other alternative hardly arises.

18. *Bud and bloom of Eden Rose; Paul's Lemon Pillar, a large flowered climber; Peace
— the absence of cerise pink on the edges of the petals illustrates the variation of the
blooms in this variety; Pink Peace (on the small side).*

19. *La Jolla, moderately large and very resistant to rain; Virgo, the very free flowering white; the outstandingly fragrant Rubaiyat in carmine; and the only really fragrant yellow, Sutter's Gold.*

In an attempt to get some idea of what one should expect I have kept a record in two successive years of the number of blooms coming from 81 varieties of hybrid teas after keeping the number of buds on each stem down to not more than two. The results ranged from five to 50 blooms; 34 varieties gave between 10 and 20: 13 varieties averaged between 21 and 25, and 17 did better than 25. At the other end 17 failed to produce 10 blooms a plant.

For those who like statistics the 780 plants involved produced each year nearly 17,000 blooms between first flowering and the end of September when counting, but not flowering, ceased; that is, an average of just over 22 blooms a plant. The number of blooms is recorded against the main varieties discussed later on.

POPULAR VARIETIES DISCUSSED

This book does not include under any heading comprehensive lists of varieties, nor are there lists of recommended varieties for various purposes. The books listed on page 180 give much and, if I may say so, excellent information. In particular the *Select List of Roses* compiled by the National Rose Society is recommended: it is included in the literature issued to members in return for a most modest subscription.

Instead, there are listed and discussed here the varieties which, judging by a fair sample of rose nurserymen's sales, are the most popular.

Publicity and salesmanship play a part; descriptions in catalogues and the views of writers in the gardening and other press exercise an influence, but it is what the man next door is growing or what the chap in the train or in the 'Local' says is good that has the most effect — and rightly so — on the purchases of the ordinary gardener. I am not saying that 'the customer is always right', but I do think that what people are buying the most of is a pretty fair measure, as regards the country as a whole, of the worthwhileness of particular varieties. These popular sellers, whose names are printed in **bold type**, are described and something is said of my own experience with them. They are also used to suggest other varieties, shown in SMALL CAPITALS, which seem to me to merit attention as one becomes more enamoured of roses. Some warnings are also included.

The descriptions will, I hope, speak for themselves, but it may help if I say that not only does foliage play an essential part in the actual growth and health of a plant but it can also enhance the beauty of the plant in general and the blooms in particular. Some varieties seem to be very aptly furnished, others less so. The quantity of foliage also varies among the specimens, but sparse foliage does not necessarily imply a poor variety, because its other qualities may be of a high order.

In view of what was said in Chapter IV about fragrance no surprise will be felt when I say that the varieties described as 'very fragrant' are those in which by general consent the fragrance can be detected even by the dullest nose. Other degrees of fragrance are ignored, but it must not be taken that no reference to this quality means that the variety is scentless.

The descriptions make on occasion comments about resistance to diseases or about predisposition to become affected by them. This unhappy subject is dealt with in Chapter XIX, from which it will be seen that the two chief diseases are black spot and mildew, and it is these two which are in mind in the present context.

Fortunately, the qualities of a rose variety, like those of an individual, are not just black or white; there are greys, too, and in assessing their values it is well to keep this in mind, especially as their values can be so much affected by locality and by the treatment they get.

I have thought it interesting, especially for those who study form and stud books, to show the parentage of the main varieties discussed (the name of the seed parent appears first). The name of the raiser and the year the variety became available in this country are also given. The latter may be of special interest in connection with what is said on page 17 about the life of a rose variety.

I add that the order in which the varieties are dealt with is not necessarily the order of their public esteem as measured by sales. Actually Ena Harkness shares with Peace the premier place and I have dealt with it first because insular prejudice makes me give precedence to a variety raised by an Englishman.

REDS

Ena Harkness. The really great red rose has yet to come: in the meanwhile this bright scarlet crimson holds first place. The foliage is satisfactory, but not particularly noteworthy. The flowers are normally of medium size and of good shape, but a bush will not infrequently throw a bloom of exhibition standard (Plate 15). The flowers stand up to rain very well: indeed, it is a variety which gives of its best in damp conditions rather than in dry. Unfortunately they do not reproduce the luscious damask fragrance of the parent Crimson Glory— for some people its scent is decidedly elusive. Equally unfortunately a percentage of its blooms hang their heads. On my measurement there were 14 blooms a bush. It can take black spot and mildew, but not badly, and is at its best on light soils rather than heavy. Of average height, i.e. 3 ft.

Raised by A. Norman from Crimson Glory × Southport: 1946

Josephine Bruce. This variety is for those who love a dark velvety crimson rose, which quite unmistakably does carry on the fragrance of Crimson Glory. It stands up well to bright sunshine and to rain. The deep green foliage resists attacks of black spot, but unfortunately it is not immune from mildew. In the ordinary way the flowers are rather smaller than those of Ena Harkness and inclined to vary in quality. The habit of growth is busy and spreading and, therefore, somewhat untidy and below average height. The flowers averaged 20. When walking round the rose garden I tend to look longer at Josephine than at Ena (Plate 16).

Raised by Bees Limited from Crimson Glory × Madge Whipp: 1952

Mme Louis Laperrière. Deep rich crimson blooms of medium size carried on shortish stems which give it its moderate height. Very fragrant. Good disease-resistant foliage. It is said to be very free flowering, but with me it has averaged only 18 blooms. Probably I have been unfortunate as there is almost universal acceptance that it is an excellent 'bedding' rose and superior to Étoile de Hollande which it has superseded (Plate 17).

Raised by Laperrière from Crimson Glory × a seedling: 1952

What of CRIMSON GLORY itself, which has helped to make the reds mentioned so far? Its fragrance is undoubted and is one of the standards against which that quality in other roses is judged. It is almost worth growing on that account alone, but its growth in general is erratic and it needs good soil and feeding to keep it going; even then it is not highly resistant to disease. I have given it up except in the climbing form which is very much more satisfactory.

There are two other crimsons which must be mentioned. KONRAD ADENAUER, Plate 20, also comes through Crimson Glory and against the opinion of better judges I prefer it to CHRYSLER IMPERIAL. Both of them tend to 'blue' as they age or are exposed to wet weather, but I regard Chrysler Imperial as the worse offender. I also find it varying in growth. On the other hand, Konrad Adenauer is stronger in the stalk, just as fragrant and for me many more blooms. It may well be that my soil suits Konrad Adenauer as it produces only a few less blooms than Ena Harkness and nearly twice as many as Chrysler Imperial. Anyway, both are worth trying if one wants to enlarge one's experience of the crimsons.

There are two reds, Red Ensign and William Harvey, of the same parentage as Ena Harkness, which the ordinary grower should eschew: they are mainly for exhibitors. The ordinary grower will also avoid Brilliant unless he wants superlative blooms at the price of some superlative mildew, and likewise Karl Herbst unless he is prepared to believe that most of our future summers will be like that of 1959. Karl Herbst produces wonderfully shaped buds, the dull scarlet flowers come freely, but they 'ball' in wet weather, or at best become discoloured. Among its redeeming points are the joy it gives to exhibitors and judges at the shows and its parentage of Perfecta, *q.v.* In the hybridizing world it is nicknamed 'The Bull'.

YELLOWS

Peace. A variety so well known that it hardly needs describing. The flowers are light or primrose yellow varying to deep yellow, with a flush of cerise pink on the edges of the petals: they come large but not very freely (18 a plant) nor very early; light pruning, however, is a help. The blooms frequently open out to look like a beautiful peony. Unfortunately there is not much fragrance. The foliage is large and of a glossy green well suited to the colour of the blooms; but it is not entirely free of black spot. Growth is tall and branching, and for this reason they should be at least 2 ft. 6 in. apart in the bed. Alone it will — lightly pruned — develop into a handsome shrub. There is a tendency for it to produce 'blind', that is, flowerless shoots; this is best dealt with by pinching them back to the next leaf stem. Stands up to rain very well. As one catalogue says — 'A connoisseur's rose which an amateur can grow.' The Peace in Plate 18 shows little or no flush on the edges of the petals and the tone of yellow is light. This illustrates how much the individual blooms can vary. Actually the bloom in question came from the climbing form (see page 76).

Raised by Meilland from Joanna Hill, Charles P. Kilham, Margaret McGredy and *R. foetida bicolor*: 1945

Sutter's Gold. This 'gold' is usually described as light orange with a pink flush. The flowers are well shaped, of medium size, carried on long stalks. Almost uniquely among yellow roses it has quite a strong

20. *Five typical globular blooms of the dark crimson and very fragrant Konrad Adenauer. Above them, right, Grand'mère Jenny, a more graceful edition of Peace and, left, two blooms of the bicoloured Tzigane. All are in the 'large' class.*

21. *The Doctor, bright silvery rose, is very fragrant. It is 'large' bloomed but 'moderately' vigorous and in the 'horses for courses' class — clearly on a good one here.*

23. Three good floribundas showing the typical trusses of bloom. They are — Rosemary Rose (top), bright carmine-crimson; Circus (left), yellow with pink and salmon shadings, and (right) the very fragrant Dearest, the mimic soft pink. (The largest bloom is well open in...

22. The hybrid tea type floribunda Queen Elizabeth, clear self pink and a very tall grower. Tucked in the middle are two blooms of the buttercup yellow Buccaneer, a tall growing hybrid tea, which makes a good companion.

fragrance. Little disbudding is needed for good blooms and the yield is just over 20 on my reckoning. The leathery, but rather sparse, dark green foliage sets off the blooms quite well: it can resist rain, disease and the conditions in London and industrial areas. Not quite pure gold, but a very good rose (Plate 19).

Raised by Swim (Armstrong Nurseries) from Charlotte Armstrong × Signora: 1950.

McGredy's Yellow. Nearly thirty years old, this rose's popularity is justified and it remains the best pure yellow. The blooms are consistently clean, well shaped, and, bless them, stand up to wet weather exceptionally well. Foliage is a weaker feature as it is rather sparse: for this reason closer planting than usual is recommended. My 25 plants average 22 blooms a plant. There is liability to black spot, but it is by no means the worst offender among the yellows. Rather above 3 ft. in height (Plates 37 and 38).

Raised by McGredy from Mrs Charles Lamplough × (The Queen Alexandra Rose × J. B. Clark): 1933

Spek's Yellow. Bright rich yellow blooms which are so numerous that they come almost in trusses and much disbudding is necessary — even so on my standard of disbudding it averages well over 30 blooms. It is tall growing, 4 ft. or over. The flowers are well shaped on long stalks, but unless the disbudding is done they are small. They stand up to rain. The leaves are shiny and in size match the flowers. They resist black spot but can be affected by mildew. Rightly among the first choices in yellows (Plate 15).

Raised by Verschuren from Geheimrat Duisberg × unnamed seedling: 1947

Lady Belper. On the information made available to me Lady Belper just gets among the best sellers: it is, however, among my first choices. The blooms, although not very large, are beautifully formed: their colour is light orange with bronze shading, but some people would think 'light orange-yellow' a better description. Anyway the colour holds well, wet or fine. There is a tendency for the second crop of flowers to come smaller than those of the first flush. This can be counteracted by a dose of quick-acting fertilizer immediately the first blooms are over. The foliage is pleasant and healthy. In most gardens the height is below 3 ft. The average number of blooms with me is 20.

Raised by Verschuren: parentage unrecorded: 1948

D

GRAND'MÈRE JENNY is a more graceful edition of Peace (its seed parent) to which it is similar in colouring, but nevertheless it is quite a distinct variety especially in its yield of blooms — 25 on my count and qualifying it for the description free flowering. Flowers usually come singly. Foliage is of the same high quality as that of Peace, but it is less tall than that variety. When walking around the rose garden I take Peace for granted but I always look specially at Grand'mère Jenny.

GOLDEN MASTERPIECE appears to sell well. It is described as a deep lemon-yellow with large free flowering blooms. It certainly did not like my old garden of sand and silt. As other people have found it disappointing too, I have not attempted to grow it in my new garden and agree with a well known nurseryman who rates it as 'Others like it more than we do'.

The apricot-yellow BEAUTÉ, although giving me only 16 blooms a bush, is another story. The long pointed flowers are graceful even though they have rather fewer petals than is desirable: nevertheless they resist the rain. The foliage is thick and leathery and a most pleasant olive green. Height is a little below average.

DOROTHY PEACH is, to paraphrase a catalogue description, a beautiful rose with large blooms, 5 in. across when open. Yellow flushed red in the bud, opening to yellow edged fawn. Vigorous growth with dark rather small foliage. My dozen have given many quite magnificent blooms — those in Plate 40 are less than average size. If your neighbourhood is free from black spot you should try it. Peace and Lydia are its parents.

DEEP PINKS AND CARMINES

Eden Rose. Deep pink with a somewhat lighter reverse, this variety leads the pinks in purchase popularity. Some people do not like its particular shade of colour: some find that it reproduces its mother's sparseness of bloom: my 32 average 18 a year. They do not mind the rain. Most of them are large and of the classical hybrid tea shape: a few, however, reveal a split centre on opening fully. As with Peace there can be blind shoots, but the glossy dark green foliage is handsome and disease-resistant. Goes to 4 ft. and a great deal over (see Plates 2 and 3).

Raised by Meilland from Peace × Signora: 1950

Rubaiyat is a rich carmine. It is a great favourite of mine on account of the strong fragrance of its flowers which come freely for so large a bloom, averaging 22 with me. The light green foliage is resistant to disease. It is the solitary British success referred to on page 24. Plate 19 by no means exaggerates its beauty if you find the colour acceptable.

Among newer roses WENDY CUSSONS, on the cerise side of pink with a flush of scarlet — a shade of colour which does not appeal to everybody — is becoming very popular on account of fragrance and healthy growth which reaches the average of 3 ft. The size of bloom can vary but, large or medium, they are invariably perfect in shape and come over a long period.

If in ordering PINK PEACE you think that you are going to get the exact counterpart of Peace in pink then you will be disappointed. Nevertheless the rather loose deep dusty pink blooms are not unattractive. They are large (the one shown in Plate 18 is on the small side) and come on stems well above average height. Incidentally it has Peace on both sides of its parentage.

JUNE PARK is a deep pink and comes from Peace and Crimson Glory: it gives very fragrant blooms of classical shape, which stand up to wet conditions very well. For these qualities it can be forgiven for its spreading and rather straggling growth.

LIGHT PINKS

Margaret. 'Clear delicate soft pink, large full flowers with high-pointed centre, free and good.' This is a 1913 rose catalogue description of another Margaret which appeared in 1903 and has long since disappeared. Save that the colour description should be 'bright pink with silvery reverse', it would do very well for the present holder of the name. To this one can add that the foliage is a pleasant dark green. No doubt the earlier Margaret had her faults and I am afraid this one has them too. She was among the leaders of the non-resistant movement in the rains of 1960 and the growth (usually well above 3 ft.), in some seasons can be curiously uneven as between one bush and another. Flower production is at an average rate of 21 and they can indeed be quite beautiful. For some reason I seem to take a more tolerant view of its weakness than I do of those of other varieties (Plate 15).

Raised by Dickson from a May Wettern seedling × Souvenir de Denier van der Gon: 1954

Monique. There appeared in 1912 (and is still available), a white suffused pink rose called Ophelia. In 1918 it 'sported' a daughter of deeper and richer colour, named Mme Butterfly, which nine years later, following its mother's lead, 'sported' a daughter — Lady Sylvia — of light pink petals with a yellow base. In 1949, true to tradition, Ophelia's grand-daughter produced Monique — in this case a seedling, not a sport: a silvery pink with rather short petals, which nevertheless lasts well. The blooms are very fragrant and average 22 on my count. The bush is vigorous and goes well over 4 ft. (Plate 16).

Some well qualified to judge consider that the 1927 LADY SYLVIA remains superior (it is often the pink variety one buys at the florist). MME BUTTERFLY is still held in high esteem and sells well in the North. Surely a wonderful family, but unfortunately, with the exception of Monique, it is addicted to malformation, if not ruination, of the buds early in the season, owing to low night temperatures and from the attention of thrips. I am afraid it is this weakness which has put them out of my garden, but the whole family may do very well in towns and industrial areas.

Monique raised by Paolino from Lady Sylvia × unnamed seedling: 1949.

Picture. That there is no record of the father and mother of this variety is a pity, as thousands of rose lovers would have wished to honour their memory. It is aptly named, for the clear bright pink blooms, although in the medium size class, are beautiful in shape and fit well into the frame of dark green foliage and shortish sturdy growth. In bloom production it is right in the top class, giving over 30 each season. It does not mind wet weather. Two snags: practically no fragrance and predilection for mildew in some areas. It is, however, a real challenge to those who would reject a scentless rose. The specimen in Plate 37 is somewhat oversize, therefore a little unfair on the two McGredy's Yellows, but it could not be resisted.

Raised by McGredy: 1932

Perfecta. Karl Herbst is not a favourite of mine but it certainly did well when it helped to produce Perfecta. This is an outstanding if, at times, a somewhat variable variety, which if not equal to Peace and Ena Harkness is well liked in that it seems to be the runner-up to those varieties in popular demand. The description is a general tone of medium rose pink, shading paler and then to yellow at the base. Plate 38 is pretty near. It has many petals, up to seventy, which reflex naturally and open gradually to make a large flower. The foliage is a handsome dark, bronzy green, and it comes very plentifully. Growth is vigorous

24. *Fan training to induce flowering by a hybrid tea climbing sport.*
25. *A low screen similarly treated, the yellow Elegance. Also shows the lateral shoots, i.e., those coming from the main stems pruned back to two or three buds.*

In the Shrub Border: 26. (Left) The bronze yellow Maigold (see also Plate 97), a continuous climber in its second year allowed to fall round Iris ochroleuca. (In the background are the three climbing Ena Harkness shown in Plate 24.)

27. (Above) Canary Bird (the species R. xanthina spontanea) developing into a good shrub rose. (See also Plate 97.)

and an outstanding feature is the way it comes up from the base of the plant. The lasting power of the blooms is outstanding. They come at the rate of 18 a plant. Less pleasant features are the slight degree of fragrance and the 'rough' buds and blooms on the first flush of flowers. This roughness has all the appearance of being the work of thrips (see page 158), but in my experience it does not appear in every season. Something over 3 ft. 6 in. tall. Overnamed, Perfecta is, however, rightly regarded as a good rose.

Raised by Kordes from Spek's Yellow × Karl Herbst: 1957.

I find LA JOLLA, in pastel shades of deep pink and yellow, so exquisite in shape and grace and so trouble-free that I willingly accept the somewhat indifferent blooms which sometimes follow the first flush. The number of blooms averages 14 and they could, if necessary, resist 24 hours of the Niagara Falls (Plate 19).

If you want a very fragrant clear rose pink of above average height with plenty of side growth try GRACE DE MONACO. The flowers come at 21 to the bush, but tend to lose their early good shape. It is decidedly above average height — with me $5\frac{1}{2}$ ft. — and I am fonder of it than I expected to be (Plate 39).

There is no hesitation in recommending MICHÈLE MEILLAND. It is appreciated by quite a few buyers already, but in my view not enough. Soft salmon-pink, the blooms, although only moderate in size, are of excellent shape and of the greatest delicacy. They come at about 26 to a bush with long stems and they do not mind the rain nor the conditions in town gardens (Plate 15).

HELEN TRAUBEL is another favourite of mine. I suspect that this is because the stems are invariably quite strong with me whereas some people hold that they are weak so that the blooms hang their heads. It has given 18 warm pink flowers a plant. Average height.

Despite the wealth of pink roses and its rather odd name VIOLINISTA COSTA must be mentioned. Perhaps it is the latter which prevents it appearing in all catalogues, but it ought not to be neglected. The colour is not easily described: orange-scarlet with gold shadings is one, but there is also something of crushed strawberry about it. Really free-flowering with a rich fragrance, but the blooms are rather loose and open quickly. One of the first roses of which I had a bed and I never regretted it. I do not think anyone would, especially those in town gardens, but look out for mildew.

For many years THE DOCTOR was a leading pink: it is still in some demand. Black spot prone, it is for London and industrial areas. But its outstanding fragrance is appreciated in both town and country. The colour is a bright silvery pink which holds well. I doubt, however, whether I should have mentioned it but for the fact that, although lightly pruned in both, it has done so much better in the heavier soil of the new garden than in the sand and silt of the old. Very much in the 'horses for courses' class (Plate 21).

SILVER LINING is a newer rose at this date and provides very pale silvery pink blooms which last a long time. They are well shaped with much fragrance, but as I have grown it for only two seasons a personal view on it must be withheld.

A much warmer pink of pronounced fragrance is MY CHOICE in pale carmine and buff. Of classical shape and vigorous growth it can be very pleasing but, owing to lack of petals, fleeting: one could wish that there were more than 16 blooms to a plant.

It was not my intention to include in this book varieties which are very new, and therefore untried, at the time of writing, to any great extent in gardens. But SUPER STAR is already such a good seller and such a good rose that it can hardly be omitted. The blooms are medium in size, but their pure light vermilion is a new colour among the hybrid teas. They are very fragrant, come freely and are well formed. The foliage is in keeping with the quality of the flowers and is highly resistant to disease (Plate 41).

Two particular warnings among the light pinks: BALLET with most attractively shaped clear pink blooms, which last well and are carried on strong upright stems. It grows vigorously. But beauty can be purchased at too great a price — in the black spot areas. Next comes a piece of real sadness. A vigorous plant with plenty of blooms, deep pink shaded with salmon and with good foliage. But I verily believe that the flowers would 'ball' even if a saucer of milk was put near them — let alone a shower of rain. What a pity it is called SIR WINSTON CHURCHILL. You should resist the name.

ORANGE, COPPER AND FLAME

Mojave. There is no doubt about the place this variety holds in the barometer of sales. In my view its popularity is well justified. Few petals, but giving delightful buds opening to small to medium sized flowers of deep orange and flame-red and of much beauty. They come on long stems at the rate of 24 to the bush. Certainly a tall upright grower as Plate 86 shows. It has bright glossy foliage which resists disease, and the blooms resist wet conditions. Despite my fond-ness for the largish classically shaped hybrid teas, Mojave is the variety I always visit first in the rose garden (and it is by no means the nearest to the house). Whether you grow roses in the north or the south, as a newcomer or otherwise, I am pretty sure that you too will not be disappointed with it (Plate 40).

Raised by Swim (Armstrong Nurseries) from Charlotte Armstrong × Signora: 1953

Mrs Sam McGredy. Much as I admire this rose and enjoy my good fortune in being able to grow it pretty well I confess to mild surprise that this variety still holds its place among the best sellers. Evidently more courses suit it than one supposed, because it is usually described as a moderately vigorous grower disliking cold and heavy conditions. But given the right treatment in the right conditions it is most re-warding. The attraction is, of course, the colour of the blooms and the beautiful foliage — perfect foils. The colour of the flowers is variously described, but bright orange-copper to scarlet is probably as good as any: their shape is superb, but for the ordinary nose there is no fragrance. Rain is resisted. Of many beautiful spring foliages the dark purple of Mrs Sam is outstanding; it grows into a bronze green. In conditions which suit it the blooms come very freely, averaging 30.

Raised by McGredy from (Donald MacDonal × Golden Emblem) × (Seedling × The Queen Alexandra Rose): 1929

Montezuma. 'Salmon-red', 'deep orange-salmon', 'camellia pink', 'light red', 'brick red'. One suspects that this variety is bought not only to determine the true colour, but also because it is something of a novelty. Left undisturbed, it produces blooms in clusters (a charac-teristic of the floribunda class), but disbudded it can, in summers like 1959, produce superb hybrid tea type blooms, which can and do win the award for 'the best bloom in the show'. But the resistance to rain is very poor and I rank it with Karl Herbst in causing disappoint-ment for the ordinary grower in wet weather. Both Montezuma and Karl Herbst have a rose in their immediate forbears, which shows the same weakness of resentment to moist conditions. There are plenty of dark green leaves, but in areas prone to black spot they are wonderful hosts to this disease. Height well over 3 ft. If you have gathered that this variety is not a favourite of mine, you are right, but I have seen some superb blooms. Try one or two plants to see what the colour really may be.

Raised by Swim (Armstrong Nurseries) from Fandango × Flora-dora: 1956

Of much the same size as Mojave but of less vivid colouring is BETTINA. Free flowering by any standard, its blooms are an orange heavily veined and overlaid with bronze. A charming rose, but unfortunately mildew is rather partial to it.

SERENADE is mentioned because of its usefulness as a decorative rose and its resistance to disease. It is orange coral, deepening at the edges of the petals. Grows vigorously and merits, in its class, more attention.

The bright orange-red OPERA seems to sell pretty well, but not so freely as one would expect from its rating by the experts. The blooms are large, well yielded at 25 to a plant, and their loveliness does not depend (for a change) on the absence of wet weather but on the ab-sence of hot. The foliage is light green and is liked by mildew and by black spot. But it is a variety said to do well in town gardens. Despite its disabilities I like it, Plate 42 shows why.

BICOLOURS

Tzigane. This is a true bicolour, that is, one side of the petal is a different colour from the reverse. The petals are bright scarlet, red inside and chrome yellow outside. The foliage, like shiny copper beech, suits these colours well, but it often looks unhappy. The growth is fairly vigorous, but somewhat below 3 ft. in height. With 21 blooms a plant, it hardly qualifies as free flowering, but to get into this bracket it needs generous feeding, especially on lighter soils. It gets a plus point for resistance to rain, but it certainly needs watching for black spot: this tendency is not noticeable in the north, where it is particularly popular. In very hard winters it is prone to 'die back' (Plate 20).

Raised by Meilland from Peace × J. B. Meilland: 1951

Cleopatra. This is another bicolour — scarlet and yellow — with medium sized flowers, having plenty of petals which stand up to the wet quite well. With me outstanding as a bloom producer, over 30 a plant. It has resisted disease quite well. Growth decidedly on the low side — less than 2 ft. I have grown it for only three years and wish I had had it earlier. Yet others, whose opinions I value, find it erratic and weak. It is, therefore, hardly surprising that its popularity surprised me.

Raised by Kordes from (Walter Bentley × Condessa de Sastago) × Spek's Yellow: 1955

Rose Gaujard. This is classed as a bicolour in National Rose Society literature, but I would put it among the carmine pinks alongside Perfecta. The blooms, which normally come singly, have a whitish base much flushed with pale pink which goes to coppery red towards the margins: in the reverse the petals are silvery. Its general colour impression is darker than Perfecta. Although a comparative newcomer it has made a real impact — and rightly so. The blooms are beautifully formed and although some may come with 'split' centres, most of the 20 per plant are very good — especially at resisting rain. The growth is very vigorous and can top 4 ft. The glossy dark green foliage is handsome and resists disease. Rose Gaujard does not sell quite as well as Perfecta, but it may be treading on its tail one day (Plate 43).

Raised by Gaujard from Peace × Opera seedling: 1958

PICCADILLY is a newcomer which seems to have got away to a good start. Described as bright scarlet on the inside and gold on the outside the colouring does not appear to be markedly different from that of Tzigane. But it is unlike, because it has a much more sparkling look, which it maintains to the very death of the flowers, whereas those of Tzigane do not die at all pleasantly. The blooms come freely. Growth is vigorous to over 3 ft. and the foliage is interesting when young because it comes as a glossy red: ageing it changes to a dark green. The flowers are a good shape, but unfortunately they are short of petals and therefore open too quickly — a great disadvantage in those hot arid summers which are so typical of our country's climate.

The hybrid tea of which I have most in my garden is a bicolour from Peace, called GRAND GALA. That I have so many is owing to the generosity of a friend, not to the outstanding qualities of the rose. Indeed, while I do not suggest that this offspring was born the wrong side of the blanket, I do not think that on this occasion Peace was giving of her best. The blooms are big, vivid scarlet inside and silvery pink outside. Unfortunately — like those of Rose Gaujard, but much more so — they come split: unlike that variety they are not happy in wet weather. When one gets a good one it is very good. But do not buy the variety: wait until it is given to you. Even so, a bowl of them, with or without split centres, can be quite striking (Plate 38).

GAIL BORDEN is, one supposes, a bicolour, but it really seems to lie between that class and those of the Rose Gaujard type in that the colour of the outer side of the petals is a somewhat paler edition of the inside. The bud colours are apricot and pale yellow moving to salmon rose inside as the blooms develop. The flowers are of excellent shape, resisting damp weather well, and a real joy, but like some other good things they are not in abundant supply — only about 12 to the bush (Plate 67).

If one wants to extend one's range of bicolours, MME L. DIEU-DONNÉ (bright carmine and yellow), and CAPRICE, also called Lady Eve Price (rose-pink with the outer petals flush•d pale yellow), have their public. Of the earliest bicolour, SULTANE, bright scarlet and deep yellow, I have some standards but they do not seem very vigorous although the flowers are showy.

WHITES

Virgo. This pure white (sometimes with a very pale flush of pink) is certainly popular. People like a white rose to set off other colours but not, I hope, with red ones for hospital patients. For general purposes Virgo is the best so far. The flowers are well formed, of medium size. In sunny weather the petals open out quite flatly and not unattractively: in wet weather they are easily the most resistant of the whites, which in this respect do not have a high reputation. With 37 blooms a plant the adjective 'prolific' is justified (Plate 19).

Raised by Mallerin from Pole Nord × Neige Parfum: 1947

The flowers of MESSAGE come much less freely: they have more petals than those of Virgo and are of better shape. I was not very successful with it when it was first available, perhaps because of too drastic pruning, and I no longer grow it.

The veteran FRAU KARL DRUSCHKI still attracts adherents and if one can get a good strain it can do very well — especially as a standard and in its late-season blooms.

There is one more hybrid tea that I must mention, because it is I suppose my favourite and because, like Crimson Glory, it provides a standard of fragrance against which other roses can be measured. GOLDEN MELODY is no more golden than a Bank of England note. Described as 'chamois yellow shading paler', I prefer 'creamy yellow' and this is why I tag it on to the whites. Many would put it with Lady Belper in the 'Buffs'. The blooms are largish, extremely well formed and rain-resistant. It can be seen at its very best in Roath Park, Cardiff, and in parts of Lancashire (Plate 39).

Looking back over the popular shopping list of hybrid teas and the varieties which I think may merit attention, I am struck with the part which Crimson Glory (including Charlotte Armstrong, one of its offspring) and Peace have played in the production of best-sellers. Breeding can provide a pointer when adventuring on one's own in the catalogues, but remember that, like varieties, strains can weaken and need new blood.

VI

Floribundas

PLATE 68 shows typical floribundas. How typical they may be and how long they will remain so is a matter of opinion. Unlike the hybrid tea group in which the varieties produce flowers of beautiful form, grace, size and substance, the floribundas in general go in for mass production of small blooms — single, double, or very double — carried in clusters or trusses at the end of a normally stout stem ('cluster' and 'truss' are synonymous and the more usual 'truss' is used in this book). This description is, however, rather over-simplified and must, I am afraid, be amplified by a little history.

There was a group of hybrid roses, dwarf with large clusters of flower, called polyanthas or poly pompons, and they were crossed with some of the single or semi-double hybrid tea roses to produce hybrid polyanthas. This hybridizing was carried out by Svend Poulsen — hence the alternative name of Poulsen roses — and resulted in a long-flowering and vigorous class admirably fitted for bedding purposes. Else Poulsen (still in some catalogues) was one of the earliest (1924) and is typical in its trusses of semi-double pink flowers. Then came crossings with fully double hybrid teas to produce small but fully double hybrid polyanthas, followed by crossings with other classes such as the hybrid musks (page 80). These crossings produced varieties giving one or two blooms on a stalk as well as in trusses, while in some the blooms were shaped like miniature hybrid teas and were so far from the original polyantha roses that some new description became necessary. 'Floribunda' was adopted by the National Rose Society to cover 'varieties which bear flowers in large trusses or clusters, in which many open at the same time, and on plants which normally grow to a height suitable for bedding purposes'.

The hybridists have continued this work. The miniature hybrid tea shaped flowers have become much larger — sometimes less shapely, sometimes more shapely, in some the number of flowers in

28. (Above) *Nevada, pale creamy white, in its second year.* 29. (Left) *Frühlingsgold — many blooms, much fragrance, but once only each year. (See also Plate 97.)* 30. (Below) *The floribunda Spartan allowed to develop into a specimen bush for the shrub border; over 6 ft.*

31. *Bad planning: unrelated space between house and boundary.* 32. *The same site with a rose and shrub garden designed by Miss Sylvia Crowe, P.P.I.L.A. (see also Plates 33 and 34).*

the trusses are somewhat fewer and with some, quite a number of flowers, each on its own stem, are carried. The pink Queen Elizabeth is one example (Plate 22). In the latest ones such as Daily Sketch (1960) the blooms are of the globular type and come quite large too.

All these variations are covered by the name 'floribunda', but 'hybrid tea type' is now being added to those varieties where it is appropriate, in descriptions issued by the National Rose Society. In the United States the designation 'grandiflora' has been used commercially and may appear in some catalogues here; but it is a misleading term which is botanically incorrect, whatever its convenience.

In general the floribundas are more, in many cases much more, vigorous than the hybrid teas. The same standards of height are used in the descriptions of the varieties dealt with later as those used for the hybrid teas (page 38), except that while 2 ft. qualifies as a short floribunda, over 4 ft. is needed to establish a claim to be tall.

The chief feature of the floribundas of all types is their ability to provide masses of bloom over long periods — with many varieties in colours of great intensity. Some of the new colours among the hybrid teas can make this claim too, for example Super Star whose pure vermilion can vie with the brightest floribundas. One would say that on the whole the floribundas are more resistant to disease — certainly they are so regards wet conditions. Moreover, they need less attention from the gardener. They are therefore ideal for the garden which needs an almost permanent splash of colour over many months, either in bed or border. Their popularity for use in public parks and on highways is due to this quality.

In saying that they need less attention one has particularly in mind that while cutting the 'dead heads' off hybrid tea roses is not a particularly arduous occupation, one can hardly bear to think of doing this with the multitudinous blooms of the floribundas. The quality of dying gracefully is therefore of particular importance in that it requires the trusses to clean themselves by shedding the petals of the dead flowers. Many a promising floribunda seedling has had to be abandoned for the fault of hanging on to its decaying petals. Some few have, however, got by. The shedding of the petals can, of course, be encouraged by flicking the branches.

A mass of colourful blooms arranged haphazardly on a floribunda may look all right far off, but it is not good enough at ordinary garden distances. For this reason the formation of the truss and the spacing of the individual flowers in it is of importance. On the one hand they must not be so crowded that they overlap or push each other out of shape; on the other hand, too sparse a distribution gives a look of general 'thinness'. Then again the truss must not be too massive for its stem so that it bends over in wet weather.

Since they are roses the floribundas have their own individuality, but it is not perhaps so pronounced as that of the hybrid teas, which on this account reign supreme for the connoisseur. This, no doubt, lies behind the complaint one sometimes hears in rose circles that 'there are too many floribundas'. How many should there be? In the catalogues referred to earlier the average number of varieties listed is around 80 compared with 120 hybrid teas, yet there is every reason to believe that for every hybrid tea bush sold there is not less than one floribunda sold too. Too many varieties or not, gardeners of all kinds have decided they want the floribunda rose and, naturally, supply follows demand.

If the criticism had been confined to the scarlet/crimson group of floribundas it would, I think, have more justification. The heavy popular demand, as revealed by the samples made available to me, however, seems to concentrate on two or three varieties. These include the leader for many years in floribunda sales and it is dealt with first.

REDS

Frensham. The semi-double scarlet crimson flowers come in quite large trusses. Usually one of the first floribundas to flower, it has the agreeable habit of giving its early blooms one or two to a stem and thus provides early cut flowers. Equally agreeable is its habit of blooming almost continuously. Another pleasing trait from the gardener's point of view, but not from that of the hybridist, is its sterility, which means that dead flowers need not be cut off because no heps will form.

The habit is vigorous to a degree and spreading too so that it needs to be planted at least 2 ft. 6 in. apart. I have had it, with light pruning, up to 7 ft. high, but something over 4 ft. would be more usual. Its armature (that is the thorns) is formidable. These qualities make it excellent for a hedge — certainly no human would willingly walk through it. The foliage is not prone to black spot, but it can take mildew erratically, one plant suffering while others in the same bed escape. Compared with some of the later reds its colours may be thought to lack sparkle. But although in the best-selling stakes Korona and Queen Elizabeth seem to be nosing ahead of it, Frensham still remains an outstanding floribunda rose in all localities.

Raised by Norman from a seedling × Crimson Glory: 1946

Elsinore and **Moulin Rouge.** It is generally, but not universally, agreed that despite quite different parentages, these two varieties are to all intents and purposes entirely similar in colour, habit and so on. My own garden experience is with the first-named and I believe that I can see a distinction, especially as regards vitality, between the two, but as to this one must keep questions of soil and cultivation in mind. But under whatever name, one has a very good floribunda. The colour is a cherry red deepening somewhat towards the edges of the petals. The flowers are semi-double, rain-resistant and carried on large well balanced trusses. The shiny foliage seldom gets disease. Growth is not so vigorous as Frensham, the height averaging about 3 ft. 6 in. (Plate 68).

Elsinore raised by Lindquist from Floradora × Pinocchio: 1958
Moulin Rouge by Meilland from Alain × Orange Triumph: 1952

A glowing scarlet-crimson called ALAIN has been available since 1946 and it is usually recommended where something not quite so vigorous as Frensham is wanted. The true alternative to that variety, however, in the opinion of a number of discerning people, is AMA, but with only two seasons' experience of it I am unable to make up my mind about it, except to say you will certainly not get an indifferent variety if you buy it — as many do.

The deep crimson scarlet RED FAVOURITE (Plate 69), with dark glossy and leathery foliage is more moderate in height than the reds already mentioned and it is useful on that account alone. Its value is enhanced by ability to resist the weather and disease. It makes excellent standards. Justifiably it sells well and can be recommended.

In 1959 I added yet another red floribunda to my collection and for that and other reasons did not give it any real attention. But the lady — LILLI MARLENE, a velvety and bright scarlet with largish flowers in big trusses — insisted on being noticed. She kept up the obtrusiveness in the deluges of 1960 and in the dry spells of 1961. Try it (Plate 70).

It is pleasant not to be under the necessity of giving a warning against particular varieties of the red, i.e., the crimson/scarlet group. Seemingly they are all good, but some are better than others.

ORANGE-SCARLETS

Korona. This bright orange-scarlet is really vivid — too much so for some people — and is easily and rightly the leader in popular

esteem in that colour group. The flowers are semi-double; they come
plentifully and continuously without regard to the weather. It is
one of the two quite outstanding floribundas in its disregard of rain.
The colour fades to a not unpleasant shade of salmon before the
petals drop. The foliage is adequate, but not entirely resistant to
black spot. All I have heard against it is that some people cannot get it
off the ground; with me new growth goes up to $4\frac{1}{2}$ ft.

HIGHLIGHT is another orange-scarlet. Its trusses are well set off
by pleasant light green foliage and are at their best in autumn.
The individual flowers, while resisting wet weather well, do not clean
themselves like those of Korona do and on this account an otherwise
excellent variety must be faulted.

ORANGEADE is a newcomer in the striking colour group. It is a
pure orange and the semi-double blooms come singly as well as in
trusses. Moderate in height — somewhat under 3 ft. — but vigorous in
growth (Plate 70).

The orange-scarlet with deep pink of THE PEOPLE can compete
on level terms with the vivid colour of Korona, but comparison ends
there as The People is one of the hybrid tea type floribundas. Its
flowers when fully open resemble a camellia. Selection of its place in
the rose garden needs care (as, indeed, do most of these bright and
vivid colours), but it can look very effective (Plate 94).

A bright glowing scarlet held by some judges in high esteem is
CONCERTO. The largish trusses carry plenty of flowers, rather on the
small side; so is the plant, which makes it useful on that account. The
foliage is light green (Plate 69).

DICKSON'S FLAME, a comparative newcomer, has been well
received not only on account of its flaming scarlet colour, but because
the semi-double flowers retain it so well. Growth is of average
height, the foliage bright and clean. I could wish, however, that the
flowers came more freely and that the trusses were spread more evenly
over the plant.

DEEP PINKS AND CARMINES

Rosemary Rose. The bright carmine-crimson flowers are large and
well-formed — sometimes described as resembling a zinnia, while
others suggest the camellia as more apt. The foliage, especially when
young, is reddish bronzy green, and is resistant to disease. The flowers
come freely and there is only a short interval between flushes (Plate 23).

33. *Sister Ann, who gives her name to the formal garden (see Plate 32) — the pedestal on which she stands and the shape of which she echoes is a dead branch of ivy.*

34. *An 'aerial' view: this and Plate 32 show the quick return from roses. Construction completed and roses, etc, planted late April 1961; photographs taken four months later.*

35. *More bad planning; main rose garden presenting a solid wall and viewers eye left at large.*

36. *Reverse view: but purpose is to show the hardiness of roses and the quick results they give. Most of those seen were planted after transfer, early in April; photograph taken end of July.*

Raised by de Ruiter from Grüss an Teplitz × a floribunda seedling: 1955

Firecracker. I make no bones about liking this variety and apparently others do too. The semi-double flowers come very freely indeed and are unique in colour — carmine shading to deep yellow. The trusses are perhaps on the small side, but the individual blooms, nearly 3 in. in diameter, are well spaced. Average height. The foliage is on the light side of green, is abundant and healthy. Most floribundas make good standards, but with me Firecracker does exceptionally well in that form (Plate 71).

Raised by Boerner (Jackson & Perkins) from Pinocchio seedling × Norma Fay seedling: 1955

For another good deepish pink I have heard AUGUST SEEBAUER constantly recommended, but I have no evidence of any ready sale. It has been available since 1950, but it has been in my garden since 1960 only. The flowers are double, well formed and have some fragrance — the trouble seems to be that while the blooms come freely the intervals between their appearances are too long — a pity.

VOGUE is another recommended variety, which does not seem to sell very freely. It is a soft deep pink and suffers from the same disability as August Seebauer—the flowers do not come often enough.

PALE VERMILION AND PALE ORANGE

Jiminy Cricket. The colour of this charmingly named variety is unusual and among the numerous attempts to describe it are — tangerine red, bright salmon-carmine, bright coral-pink, strawberry-orange and coppery salmon. Get some and make your own estimate. The foliage is a most pleasant coppery red and, within its somewhat below average height, the growth is vigorous. The flowers come freely in trusses rather smaller than most. It is a favourite of mine and I am glad it sells well and can abide plenty of rain (Plate 68).

Raised by Boerner (Jackson & Perkins) from Goldilocks × Geranium Red: 1955

Fashion. Rich orange-salmon, but so much more restrained than the 'oranges' that coral-pink describes more accurately its almost pastel shade. The flowers are on the large size and come freely in good trusses. The growth is only moderate and it does not often pass the

E

2½ ft. mark. Crimson Glory seems to have transmitted its rather indifferent foliage, but a bed of Fashion is quite quite beautiful — and many people must know it. I had such a bed — two dozen of them — and on returning from holiday one September the rose garden was found to be a blaze of colour and the bed of Fashion a blaze of rust, a disease to which the variety is very susceptible (page 161). I tried a standard of it which in the dry summer of 1959 quickly died for no apparent reason. Do not let my misfortunes deter you from following the thousands who grow Fashion successfully in rust-free areas.

Raised by Boerner (Jackson & Perkins) from Pinocchio × Crimson Glory: 1947

If, however, one does fear rust and can, for rose garden purposes, equate 'coral-pink' with 'light vermilion with a golden glow', then go for ANNA WHEATCROFT with largish single and semi-double flowers, set off by dark green foliage. Its growth is bushy, its height rather under average. It is a good substitute.

SPARTAN is one of the earliest examples of the hybrid tea type of floribunda — each flower like a miniature hybrid tea, the size of which can, of course, be increased by disbudding. The colour is rich salmon to light red. With me it grows to well over 5 ft. The foliage is not too impressive and this may be accounted for by the fact that Fashion was its pollen parent (but I have never seen rust on it). It seems to sell pretty well, but I am sure that it would do much better, and deservedly so, if wet weather was resisted more effectively.

LIGHT PINKS

Now let us rest our eyes from the strident and the glaring by having a look at the pinks. Away ahead of them all is:

Queen Elizabeth. This is a hybrid tea type of floribunda. The clear self pink flowers come both singly and in small trusses. They are large — up to 4 in. — on practically thornless stems (Plates 22 and 96). The foliage is a pleasant green and resists disease: I could wish the blooms resisted wet weather rather better than they do. They are said to come freely. But in my experience they are not as free as all that: there are plenty of hybrid teas providing a larger total of blooms in the season. About its height there can be no dispute: it is just plain tall, so much so that it is best at the back of a border, whether of roses or other flowers: a bed of Queen Elizabeth is not recommended as they tend to hit one under the chin. One should certainly not be without this variety — its colour is charming.

Raised by Lammerts from Charlotte Armstrong × Floradora: 1955

DAINTY MAID has, I am sorry to say, rather dropped out of the running these days in popular estimation. But it is still in the catalogues (where it first appeared 25 years ago) and, in my view, rightly so. Its pale rose-pink flowers are delightful, but they do not seem to have enough petals for modern taste — they are singles. Well above 4 ft. in height. With Korona it is the leader among the rain-resistant floribundas (Plate 72).

What a nuisance mildew can be. Did it not exist I would wholeheartedly recommend UNITED NATIONS as the best pink floribunda— its pink is shaded deep yellow at the centre. Grows to under 3 ft. only, but it goes on flowering in an unassuming way which cannot but please, and dies so gracefully. You will be well rewarded if you are willing to spray against that mildew (Plate 71).

Against my self-imposed restriction I mention, as a balance to Super Star, a 1960 floribunda. I have selected DEAREST, because it is for me a really delightful shade of pink — pale and soft and to be preferred to that of Queen Elizabeth, which is saying much. The flowers when open are largish, over 3 in., quite flat, and remind one of the old garden roses in both shape and fragrance. The foliage is a pleasant dark green. Naturally there is a snag, but in this case I willingly accept it: Dearest does not take too kindly to rain (Plate 23).

YELLOWS

A frequent statement in rose circles is that there is, as yet, no really good yellow floribunda—countered quite often by the remark 'What is wrong with using the hybrid tea Spek's Yellow (page 49) undisbudded?' Judging by the sample of sales there is certainly a strong demand for what is available.

Allgold. An unfading golden yellow, whether in sun or rain; the flowers come freely and, although not as large as those on some floribundas, are of good shape. The foliage is on the small size, but is bright and tough. Mildew and black spot pass it by and rain cannot harm it. Normally not above 2 ft. in height. I do not see much wrong here: nor do the public (Plate 94).

Raised by Le Grice from Goldilocks × Ellinor Le Grice: 1956

Faust. Not a pure yellow because the golden yellow petals are shaded pink as the flowers mature. It is of the hybrid tea type and very vigorous: in relation to Allgold it is certainly Big Klaus.

Foliage is a pleasant deep green. It stands up to wet weather but not so well to mildew. Some people find this to be very bad, but for my part although it has misbehaved badly on this account on two occasions in the first year after planting, thereafter there has been hardly a trace.

Raised by Reimer Kordes from Masquerade × Spek's Yellow: 1956

Goldilocks. Apparently this variety still sells well, but I regard it as clearly inferior to Allgold and Faust. The trouble with it is that the flowers come a good rich yellow but soon fade to cream and a not very pleasant one at that. In its bush form I would leave it alone, but its climbing sport (page 78) is another story.

Raised by Boerner (Jackson & Perkins) from an unnamed seedling × Doubloons: 1954.

CHANELLE is hardly a yellow as its general effect is buff pink (Plate 69). The blooms come in trusses, but are miniature hybrid tea in shape. The growth is robust, and somewhat above average height. The foliage, large and outstanding, is resistant to disease: a group of three in my garden are wrapped round by the long branches of Conrad F. Meyer (page 83) which are smothered with rust and black spot. There is no trace whatsoever on Chanelle, and not a speck of mildew on either of them. It seems from the sales that I am not the only one who is impressed by this comparative newcomer.

YELLOW-FLAME AND BICOLOURS

Now for a rather miscellaneous group wherein the colours are so varied or so changeable that they elude any precise category.

Masquerade. Most aptly named: the buds are deep yellow, changing to pink when they open and then gradually going to deep red. As this process is continuous all the colours are present on the bush at the same time. The trusses are large, they come freely, the growth is vigorous, the foliage is excellent and not prone to disease. It is very popular. I do not like it much and grow it only because I feel that I ought to (Plate 95).

Raised by Boerner (Jackson & Perkins) from Goldilocks × Holiday: 1950

37. *Picture is a real picture. The larger bloom is, however, out of character as it is indeed 'large' whereas it should be 'medium'. It is thus unfair on the two blooms of McGredy's Yellow which ranks as 'large' — see Plate 38.*

39. *Deeper colour is often seen in September. Golden Melody looks golden. Grace de Monaco is deeper too.*

38. *Beauty can be full blown. Perfecta and the bi-coloured Grand Gala with McGredy's Yellow in the background.*

Circus. To me this is in every way a more restrained Masquerade, and therefore to be preferred. The colour is yellow with pink and salmon shadings but it varies considerably, especially as the flowers age. It can also vary as between plants. The flowers are well formed hybrid tea type and fit into the trusses admirably, but there might be more of them. Rather on the short side — about 2 ft. 6 in. The deep green leaves resist disease quite well. Another one for good marks in resistance to wet (Plates 23 and 69).

Raised by Swim (Armstrong Nurseries) from Fandango × Pinocchio: 1955.

Sweet Repose. The flowers of this variety are on the large side — about 3 in. — and of good shape. 'Light pink shading yellow' or 'light yellow and pink' are used to describe their colour, but it is not quite as simple as that, as the general effect is that of a bicolour, while during maturity the pink deepens to crimson. The foliage is a most suitable deep green; the height is above rather than below 3 ft. My wife's favourite floribunda. I like it too and so do many others (Plate 71).

Raised by de Ruiter from Geheimrat Duisberg × a polyantha: 1956

SHEPHERD'S DELIGHT, orange-red shading to yellow towards the base, and SALUTE, deep rose shading to yellow, are both popular and well worth growing. They are very vigorous; both have good trusses with well spaced flowers. Salute has medium and Shepherd's Delight has dark green foliage. Both are disease-resistant. As might be expected from the colour descriptions the all-over effect when in full bloom is, however, different, the rose colouring tending to predominate in Salute and the yellow in Shepherd's Delight. In my garden the former is usually the first floribunda in flower, but the latter goes on longer in the autumn.

A new bicoloured floribunda which I feel merits more attention is TAMBOURINE, the flowers of which are fairly full and are cherry red shading to yellow at the base, on the reverse the petals are a pale orange: perhaps the tones are a little on the dull side, but a pleasant change. It is very vigorous, grows up to 4 ft., stands any kind of weather and disease, and should not be passed by.

WHITES

Whether or not there is a really good yellow floribunda may be debated, but there has been little doubt about the lack of an outstanding white. This is clearly evidenced by the demand for:

Iceberg. A very vigorous grower, over 4 ft., with pure white flowers following pinkish buds, which come freely. Rain is resisted and so is disease. Foliage is a pleasant light green. The general effect is rightly described as dainty. We could do with some more floribundas of this kind in other colours (Plate 70).
    Raised by Kordes from Robin Hood × Virgo: 1958

IVORY FASHION came out in 1957 and seems to be catching on. The colour is creamy white deepening to near apricot towards the base of the petal — the general effect is ivory white. The young blooms are miniature hybrid teas in shape and are carried in medium sized trusses. Fashion is the pollen parent but I have yet to see the rust. I like it very much (Plate 68).

VII

Climbers

There is much variation in the rose catalogues in the headings covering
the title of this chapter. Here are a few — 'Rambler Roses'; 'Large
flowered climbers'; 'Everblooming Climbing Roses'; 'Ramblers';
'Wichuraiana and other Rambling Roses'; 'Repeat flowering Climbing Roses'; 'Perpetual Climbing Roses'; 'Climbing Sports'; 'Climbing Hybrid Teas'; 'Climbers and True Wichuraiana'; 'Climbing and
Rambling Roses'; 'Climbing Roses'.

These headings appear in various combinations covering different
sections, sometimes two, occasionally three. Only two of a sample
dozen of catalogues produced exactly the same headings. They are
all correct in their way, but I well remember how difficult it was to
sort it all out in my early days of interest in roses. My sympathy is
with the nurserymen who, giving up the struggle to get the various
classes under their correct headings, fall back on the simple title of
'Climbers', list their varieties alphabetically and then describe the
characteristics of each. This may mean a certain amount of repetition,
but it is certainly less frightening and, I think, more helpful for the
customer. However, catalogue life must be dealt with as it is.

For many people, and it certainly was so with me, the terms
'rambler rose' and 'climbing rose' mean the same thing. But in fact
they do not. A rambler is a climber; a climber is not necessarily a
rambler. The ramblers are but one of a variety of climbing roses.
They have been mainly produced from the wild or species rose
R. wichuraiana, some, however, come from *R. multiflora*, (hence the
heading mentioned above 'True Wichuraiana'). The main characteristics of the ramblers are rampant growth and small flowers coming in
one glorious burst of bloom lasting up to five weeks in late June or
early July. Thereafter they need pruning back, overhauling and the
vigorous new growth, which will carry the blooms in the next year,
tying in. This is excessively laborious and unpleasant.

The old and well known American Pillar and Dorothy Perkins are typical rambler roses. In favourable circumstances some one or two give a flicker of further flowers in September; the lovely Albertine is an example, but it is only a flicker. As usual, however, there is invariably an exception to a general rule. Although of true wichuraiana parentage, New Dawn is everblooming and its blush pink flowers are for many people a continual joy. In the catalogues New Dawn often appears under other headings than 'Ramblers', while under that heading other small-flowered climbers such as Paul's Scarlet are included. This does not matter much provided one gets to know, in one way or another, what to expect from them.

Before discussing the 'climbers' in contrast to the 'ramblers' it might, perhaps, be useful to be clear about what is meant by such expressions as 'perpetual', 'continuous', 'everblooming', 'recurrent', 'repeat flowering'. The first three, I take it, mean the same thing: namely, that the climbing rose so described will normally have a display of blooms — varying very much in quantity — throughout the growing season, usually June to October in the south, but shorter in the north. Hereafter I use 'perpetual' or 'continuous' to describe such performers. 'Recurrent' and 'repeat flowering', however, mean, I imagine, that after one flush of bloom there is an interval followed by another flush. These expressions are here so used. An example of repeat flowering is provided by the climbing sports (see page 75) from the hybrid teas, which like their bush counterparts give a second flush of bloom early in September. Unlike their counterparts, however, the second crop of the climbers is almost invariably nothing like so large as the first.

There is one other term which calls for explanation. If a rose variety of any kind gives one crop or flush of bloom only, as for example the ramblers, it is usually described as 'summer flowering'. An odd kind of expression which one can only assume is founded on the fact that in this country, whatever the calendar may prescribe as constituting summer — June 21 to September 20 — weather of that description is of remarkably short duration. 'Summer flowering' is sometimes modified by the addition of 'some repeat'.

The heading 'Large Flowered Climbers' covers a recognized class of climbers consisting of the climbing sports of the hybrid teas on the one hand and, on the other, a 'diversity of creatures'. It has been mentioned that the climbing sports do not give freely of blooms in the second flush, but there are agreeable features on the other side of the account. Some varieties are easier to grow as climbers, and sometimes the quality of the blooms is much better than those from bushes. Examples are Mrs Sam McGredy and Crimson Glory. Moreover, the climbing sports tend to come into bloom quite a bit earlier than their bush counterparts, and they are usually ahead of the other kinds of climbers.

In their diversity the other Large Flowered Climbers cover a wide range from the celebrated Paul's Lemon Pillar (summer flowering only) of hybrid tea form (Plate 18), the single crimson red Allan Chandler (repeat flowering), to newcomers such as Danse du Feu, and a group bred from R. *kordesii* by the hybridist, Kordes.

R. *kordesii* arose as a sport (technically known as a mutation) of a seedling which came from a cross between R. *rugosa* and a R. *wichuraiana* hybrid. For those who understand such things, it may be of interest that the sport took the form of chromosome doubling: hence R. *kordesii* is a tetraploid. The kordesii climbers have been bred by crossing R. *kordesii* with various other roses including ramblers, hybrid teas and floribundas.

After the Ramblers and the Large Flowered Climbers come the rest of the climbers and a very large rest it is too, with some very beautiful and useful varieties in it, which we must lump together as 'other climbers'. These include the relatively few climbing sports from the floribundas, such as Goldilocks (although these sometimes appear in the catalogues among the ramblers). The single primrose yellow Mermaid and the nearly-100-year-old Bourbon variety Zephirine Drouhin are usually to be found among 'other climbers'.

To sum up: **The Ramblers** then are strictly those climbers bred from R. *wichuraiana*, but the group sometimes includes those bred from R. *multiflora* and it often covers other small-flowered climbers. With one or two notable exceptions the varieties in this group are summer flowering.

The Large Flowered Climbers contain (1) The climbing sports from the hybrid teas; (2) Other large flowered varieties of wide and varied parentage; for the most part they are perpetual flowering, but there are some summer flowerers only.

The Other Climbers sweep up what remains — a pretty large and varied group too.

The following are the varieties which seem to be mostly in demand. As in other sections they are not in numerical order, but it is interesting to note that examples of all the various kinds I have tried to elucidate seem to be in favour.

RAMBLERS

Albertine has buds of a lovely reddish salmon opening to copper pink. Trusses of very fragrant flowers are produced in one flush, but what a flush. I have seen a slight flicker of bloom in the early autumn. The armature is very fierce and so is the growth. A Cox's Orange Pippin in my old garden which had never done at all well was used as a pillar for an Albertine. The way it threaded itself through the apple foliage and revealed its blooms was quite delightful. It shook up the Cox, too, because it forthwith gave a wonderful crop and so continued. This is an illustration of one way to grow ramblers — if not of how to get a Cox's Orange Pippin to bear fruit — to me they look so much more natural than when on an artificial arch or on a fence.
Raised by Barbier from *R. wichuraiana* × Mrs A. R. Waddell: 1921

New Dawn is pale or blush pink and is a perpetual flowering sport (1930) from another wichuraiana rambler, Dr W. van Fleet, but it is not nearly so rampant as the parent. Indeed, it is often described as a pillar rose: mine seem to do rather better than that. New Dawn is usually out early in the season and it is one of the last climbers to cease. An added attraction is its habit of blooming throughout its height, at any rate during the first flush of flowers.

Emily Gray is rightly noted for its dark, practically evergreen foliage. Left to itself to ramble with some support it produces an attractive and efficient hedge. Compared with the other ramblers it is somewhat slow in establishing itself, but once away it really goes. The flowers are pale golden yellow. They come more freely if pruning is kept to a minimum. Summer flowering only.
Raised by Williams from Jersey Beauty × Comtesse de Cayla: 1916

With so many more beautiful and better climbing roses now available one can only suppose that some kind of folk lore keeps AMERICAN PILLAR still in the public mind — it is now sixty years old. Admittedly it is very vigorous and the large clusters of single blooms make a great show once a year. But the colour is a hard bright rose with a white eye and when one realises how much pruning has to follow its display, it just does not seem worth it. Moreover, it can do one really proud by way of mildew — illustrating a point that the ramblers, owing to this predisposition and to their vigour, are best not grown on walls, whether of houses or elsewhere.

Raised by Dr van Fleet from (*R. wichuraiana* × *R. setigera*) × a red hybrid perpetual: 1902

For DOROTHY PERKINS, another apparently still in favour, re-read the foregoing with the substitution of 'small rose pink double flowers' and underline mildew.

Raised by Jackson & Perkins from *R. wichuraiana* × Mme Gabriel Luizet: 1901

Paul's Scarlet Climber — not a 'rambler', just a 'climber', but it is convenient to deal with it here. Probably best used as a pillar rose, it can, however, unlike the ramblers, be used on a wall, where, mildew-free, it should be watched for black spot. Unlike New Dawn it does not produce blooms down to the base, but pruning two or three stems to graduated heights can counteract this fault. The blooms are bright scarlet crimson. Summer flowering with a later flicker. I found it quite vigorous, especially on light soil, but in spite of its popularity it has never been much of a favourite of mine.

Raised by Paul from Paul's Carmine Pink × Soleil d'Or: 1915

In 1928 it was crossed with American Pillar to give CHAPLIN'S PINK CLIMBER, which is a favourite of mine and of others too. It can be thoroughly recommended provided one keeps in mind that its apparently innocuous 'soft pink' is really a rather hard 'bright pink', so that one has to be particularly careful in choosing its neighbours. Its golden yellow stamens, however, go very well with the semi-double flowers. A pity there is only one flush of flowers.

LARGE FLOWERED CLIMBERS
CLIMBING SPORTS OF HYBRID TEAS

Clg. Ena Harkness, which I find to be outstanding in bloom production in the first flush and does better than most later on. Perversely, because it matters less, blooms with weak stems seem to be less frequent than on the bushes.

Clg. Crimson Glory is rightly more popular than in its bush form; both foliage and blooms seem better. The strong fragrance is no stronger but the climbing form can bring it closer to one's nose. Seeing the number of varieties which have Crimson Glory blood in them it would be a graceful gesture to grow it on that account alone, but it justifies its place on its own merits.

Clg. Mrs Sam McGredy can give much satisfaction in climbing form and provide some really breathtaking blooms. For those who have difficulty in growing the bush form I would suggest a trial of the climber.

In general the climbers — especially the sports — do not establish themselves so quickly as the bush roses. One cannot expect much, if anything, in the first year and nothing very spectacular in the second. SHOT SILK, light carmine shaded orange salmon, an old favourite in its bush form, can be an exception to the general rule as a climber. One of mine really shot up and took some beautiful blooms through a small window, which is usually kept open, into a small room, where its strong fragrance was much appreciated.

The climbing form of the deep red ÉTOILE DE HOLLANDE has been recommended for over thirty years on account of its fragrance, colour and vigour. On light soil against a south-west wall I could do little or nothing with it. On the other hand I have great praise for the old MME CAROLINE TESTOUT as a climber, because although its warm pink is not to everybody's liking its vigour and notably good repeat flowering cannot but please.

'Climbing Peace gleams on a dark stone wall'. I am afraid that the source of this extract was not noted. I would not doubt the assertion any more than one would dispute that 'the evening star gleams in the sunset sky'. One star — and one bloom of Peace. Whatever Climbing Peace may do elsewhere it will in general only disappoint in this country. Do not buy it unless you have a passion for foliage or you have a dark stone wall on which you wish a single bloom to gleam. The Peace in Plate 18 was my 1961 bloom.

OTHER LARGE FLOWERED CLIMBERS

The other large flowered climbers in demand are examples of the modern production of climbers, most of which in return for less rampant growth give a fairly continuous display of bloom.

Danse du Feu. A climbing example of the current appetite for bright colours: it is a vivid orange scarlet. I have found it an outstanding

40. *Serenade (left) and the popular Mojave (right) are typical 'decoratives'. The yellow Dorothy Peach can give magnificent blooms of classical shape and size.*

41. *Beautiful throughout a long life the blooms of Super Star are pure light vermilion of medium size and perfect form.*

42. *Opera is good in the bed and above it. This standard is in its second season and promises to develop a fine head.*

43. *(Right) Rose Gaujard after over six hours of steady rain — still immaculate and still very fragrant.*

exception to the slow starting rule as it gave an excellent crop of medium-sized blooms as well as new growth from the base in the first year. Usually more than its predicted 8 ft. in height, it has also given lateral spreads of 6 ft. on either side and flowers for five months with hardly any interrruption. If black spot is about, however, it will not pass it by.

Raised by Mallerin from Paul's Scarlet Climber × unnamed *R. multiflora* seedling: 1954

Golden Showers. A fitting companion for Danse du Feu as regards its flowering season. A true golden yellow, the buds are long, but soon open up to the semi-double flower. Unlike Danse du Feu it does not in my experience grow away very quickly. Out of some half-dozen only one was up to 7 ft. in the first season. The others remained large shrubs giving a constant supply of blooms. Golden Showers is particularly well grown in the Queen Mary Rose Garden in Regent's Park, London.

Raised by Lammerts from Charlotte Armstrong × Capt. Thomas: 1957

The yellow ELEGANCE seems to give great satisfaction to all who grow it: it does so to me too. The large flowers come in great abundance on longish stems late in May or in the first half of June, but one has a fruitless search for anything later. I regret very much not having grown it before 1959 although it was available twenty-two years earlier. A group of three have covered 24 ft. of wire fencing at a height of 5 ft. in two years (Plate 25).

ALLEN CHANDLER has been considered by a number of people, since 1924, to be worth growing. A vivid scarlet in semi-double large flowers, it seems best on a pillar. During ten years it has not made a great impression on me. My wife likes it very much.

I am sorry to confess failure with GUINÉE, a very dark scarlet of much the same tone as that of Josephine Bruce, especially as it is so fragrant. Three plants from three different sources have been tried, but they have either not grown at all or petered out after a couple of years. Other people speak highly of it, especially as it blooms freely and almost perpetually.

Hamburger Phoenix. This kordesii climber has crimson semi-double flowers in clusters and they are well set off by the darkish glossy green foliage. Although described as a pillar rose it gives a good lateral spread. 1955

Leverküsen is a golden yellow twin to Hamburger Phoenix, but the flowering is recurrent rather than continuous and the second blooming not so prolific as the first. The colour loses some of its gold in hot weather, but as that condition is hardly frequent it does not matter much (Plate 96). On the whole for a tallish yellow pillar rose I prefer High Noon. It flowers almost continuously from early June to December, but is less free with its foliage than Leverküsen.

ZWEIBRÜCKEN is a deep crimson kordesii with largish flowers coming in good-sized trusses or clusters. It is very vigorous with me.

DORTMUND is the kordesii climber for those that like single flowers. Their red is enhanced by a white eye. It has all the other features of the group, but I confess I bought some under the impression that it was a modern shrub rose. At the end of the first season each of them had shoots up to 11 ft. long, so I concluded that I had mis-informed myself. The truth is that Dortmund, like some of the other Kordesii climbers, can be kept pruned back to form a bushy shrub. *Per contra* some of the shrubs raised by Kordes (see Chapter VIII) will, left unpruned or lightly pruned, frequently make effective pillar roses.

OTHER CLIMBERS

Now for the remainder of the climbers. Miscellaneous indeed, but they include some very excellent varieties.

Zéphirine Drouhin, a centenarian in age, a Bourbon in variety, has semi-double flowers in a bright carmine pink with much fragrance. Sometimes and rightly called the Thornless Rose. I should not have said it was an early variety but 1961 saw mine out, in an admittedly very early spring, by the first week in May. According to the books July is its best time, with intermittent blooms thereafter. Very worthwhile—better perhaps on a wire fence than against a wall? It can also be pegged down to form a shrub.

Clg. Goldilocks. The floribundas do not seem to sport into the climbing form nearly so frequently as the hybrid teas do. As a bush rose one would not rate Goldilocks very highly as its small rich yellow flowers pale down to a not very attractive cream and they do not clean themselves very readily as they die off. In some odd way, however, one does not notice these deficiencies in the climbing, or rather pillar, form where large clusters come freely and recurrently. Usually described as moderately vigorous, but with me at heights of between 4 ft. and 9 ft., it covers 7 ft. in each direction. Evidently many others find it satisfactory too.

Maigold was raised by Kordes in 1953 and although not from *R. kordesii* it has the character of that group — free and continuous flowering with large, if unshapely when full, blooms. Its buds, however, are very pleasant. My experience is limited, so far, to two seasons. The first produced no blooms; the second showed Maigold among the very earliest climbers to come out. It is another variety I wish had come my way much sooner. To make up for this omission the flowers of Maigold have been included in Plate 97 and Plate 26 shows it in the shrub border where it is allowed to droop without support.

Mermaid has a fair sales popularity but on such descriptions as 'one of the finest of all climbers' and 'supremely beautiful' one would expect it to occupy a much higher place in esteem, especially as it requires little or no attention by way of pruning. One suspects that on the whole single flowered roses are not popular these days and the zest for quick results makes people impatient at the long time it takes to move. When it does there is no holding it. Plate 48 shows Mermaid after three seasons against my new house; its height is just over 6 ft. The specimen against my old one covered 150 sq. ft. up to the gutters in eight years and was a sight well worth waiting for. The single flowers are primrose yellow with amber stamens and come fairly continuously. The stems are very brittle: the thorns are vicious.

VIII

Shrub Roses

Under this heading the catalogues mostly include a miscellaneous collection of roses, a regular rag bag, but full of great beauty and usefulness. Some catalogues, however, subdivide the title and a typical sample shows what this chapter will cover:

'Shrub Roses'; 'Moss Roses'; 'Species Roses'; 'Musk Roses'; 'Hybrid Musks'; 'Sweet Briars'; 'Rugosa Roses'; 'Scotch Briars'; 'Specimen Bushes'.

This group is usually at the end of the catalogues and readers who by the time they reach it feel mentally or financially exhausted may, perhaps, be excused. Those who approach it with the attitude that the contents must be dull and out-of-date cannot be excused. Both groups if they pass it over will be missing something worthwhile for their gardens, and as for out-of-dateness practically all rose nurserymen offer vivid shrub roses introduced since the war. Other readers may be deterred owing to an idea that shrub roses are only for the large garden. As to this: if I had a garden which could take one shrub only it would be a shrub rose as there are so many to choose from which would give months of continuous bloom, while many of them can be kept pruned back to a convenient size. Amongst the shrub roses, too, one can also find soft pastel shades as a relief from the strident colours of the more modern types.

HYBRID MUSKS

We will begin, however, with a group which under the name hybrid musks contains colours to suit all tastes: the older members showing the pastel shades and the new fellows the vividness of the present day. The knowledgeable in these matters hold that the musk rose — *R. moschata* — in them is so remote as to be meaningless. Others say that whatever the claim the older varieties may have to be called hybrid musks, the newcomers certainly have none. Yet others hold that, at

Looked at closely it will be seen that the maiden bush (44) is dried out and shrivelled. Planted it will be unlikely to survive. The remedy is to bury it completely a spit deep (45); water and label the grave (46). Disinterred (47) 10 days later it will be found to be completely restored.

48. *Mermaid is an excellent climber, but one needs patience. The one here (on chimney breast) is only 6 ft. after three seasons.*

49. *Bad planting: 'union' of tree (left) is 2 in. above instead of at ground level (right). Photographed two years later.*

any rate, the fragrance of some of them is reminiscent of musk. The older ones are sometimes criticized on the ground that no matter what colour they may be at first, the flowers all develop into a uniform pale pink. Even if this be true, and it is not noticeably so to me, their virtues quite make amends.

The hybrid musks well illustrate the difficulty the nurseryman may have in sorting out the shrub groups in his catalogue, and I suggest that if you do not find a variety under the heading you expect, other groups should be looked at before it is decided that your rose nursery-man does not carry it.

The earlier issues of the hybrid musks included some fifteen varieties but only those commonly offered, and they are on the whole the best of them, are mentioned.

PENELOPE is pale pink shaded salmon and the musk fragrance is claimed for it. The small semi-double flowers open to show the sta-mens: they come in large trusses, with flushes in early summer and early autumn. The foliage is glossy. Just lightly tipped it will grow to over 5 ft. (some of mine are over 8 ft.), or it can be pruned in the ordinary way to produce a medium sized plant for the bed. In general Penelope typifies the description of the group that they are in a way more refined floribundas.

MOONLIGHT is a taller grower than most and produces lemon-white flowers similar in shape to those of Penelope, but in smaller trusses. It is noted for its foliage which can come a most agreeable mahogany red.

VANITY has blooms, almost single in formation, of bright pink. With rather less foliage than others, it is, however, very vigorous and on the tall side.

FELICIA is also pink, a salmon tone. The flowers are more shapely than some of the others and the foliage is large.

BUFF BEAUTY, perhaps because it grows smaller than the others — about 4 ft. — seems to have been neglected and it does not appear in many catalogues; but it is certainly worth trying as the blooms are full-petalled, rather like a hybrid tea in shape, and a pleasing apricot yellow.

WILHELM is a rich crimson, with semi-double flowers which come almost continuously. A tall grower. It came out in 1934 from Kordes and in 1950 gave a sport in bright scarlet, sometimes described as hunting pink, called WILL SCARLET, which is less vigorous than Wilhelm. Neither of these has become as well known as the follow-

F

ing very bright coloured trilogy of Kordes which became available in 1949–50.

Penelope, Felicia, and Will Scarlet appear in Plate 98.

BERLIN has single flowers of vivid orange scarlet showing attractive golden stamens, which come freely in floribunda-like trusses. Scheduled to grow up to 5 ft., it can, like its companions, do very much better.

ELMSHORN has a very distinct colour, a light crimson not always easy to place with other colours. To my discomfort it does not go alongside Danse du Feu (see page 109). Its small flowers may appeal to some for the very regular pattern of the petals.

BONN is also described as orange-scarlet and is an illustration of the somewhat wide range of tones covered by that description, because Bonn is far from a double version of Berlin. The foliage, in common with the two others, is light green which suits the colours of the flowers. It is easily my favourite of the three.

Another common feature, and an important one, is that although described as growing to about 5 ft. they can all do much better than that and can be treated as pillar roses, as some are in my garden (Plate 96). For this reason some catalogues include them under the heading of 'Climbers'.

MOSS ROSES

Most catalogues will include a few of the moss roses with their lax but graceful growth, large-leaved foliage and, of course, the moss-like growth covering the buds. The COMMON (OR PINK) MOSS is the most commonly seen in the lists. It is particularly noted for its globe-shaped flowers, which as they open up show a 'button' eye in the centre. Although growing to about 4 ft. in height its stalks are much longer than that, bending over very gracefully. Unfortunately, there is only one crop of bloom.

The white variety which was the matter of contention between Sergeant Cuff and the Gardener is known variously as the WHITE BATH, WHITE MOSS and CLIFTON MOSS. Its correct name seems to be SHAILER'S WHITE MOSS and it has all the characteristics of the Common Moss: this is not surprising as it sported from it. The White Moss should not be confused with another white variety, BLANCHE MOREAU, which despite the recurrence of its many petalled blooms and popularity in the catalogues is not, in my view, of the same quality as the White, with or without a Bath.

Planting: 50. Three-gallon bucket of damp peat moss in barrow for convenience of mixing in — 51. a double handful of meat and bone meal. 52. Handful of mixture added to loose soil at bottom of hole. 53. Plant put in and handful of mixture added.

Planting: 54. A handful of soil is followed by one of mixture and so on — 55. as hole becomes full firm in from outside — 56. towards the plant — 57. then tidy up the soil surface to leave it neat.

WILLIAM LOBB is also frequently offered. Its flowers are mauve to lavender grey and there is plenty of moss on the buds. Height is about 6 ft. and the description 'gaunt' is apt. I like it sufficiently to wish that it had more than one crop of bloom.

The light crimson Baron de Wassenaer appears in many catalogues carrying moss roses, but it is really rather undistinguished and lacks the essential feature of its kind — a sufficiency of moss. On the other hand the blush pink and perpetually flowering MOUSSELINE (or Alfred de Delmas), with dense foliage, ought to be much more freely available.

RUGOSAS

R. rugosa typica, the Japanese wild rose, which in addition to being a shrub rose in its own right has produced, in one way or another, a most useful collection of shrubs. These flower quite early in the season and their very names, such as Blanc Double de Coubert at one end and Schneezwerg at the other, are irresistible. Unfortunately the ordinary run of catalogue does not offer a big selection.

BLANC DOUBLE DE COUBERT has semi-double pure white blooms, cup shaped and of much fragrance; they come intermittently. It is said to grow to 6 ft., but with me it is taking its time. The foliage is bright with deep veins and is typical of many in the group. Already a favourite of mine.

SCABROSA. One can think of more attractive names, but the largish single magenta flowers are followed by large attractive heps (Plate 100). In two years it has progressed well towards its ultimate height of 4 ft. An added attraction is the perpetual flowering.

CONRAD F. MEYER is a tall and gaunt grower, scheduled for 7 ft., but it is in two years 10 ft. with me. The advice to put it at the back of the border with other shrubs in front is clearly sound. To this I would add a further piece: do not put it in at all in rust and black spot country. In 1961 it provided me with my second experience of rust and the material for Plate 99. The flowers are silver pink (nearer to the silver than the pink) and hybrid tea type in shape.

If RED GROOTENDORST is seen in a catalogue it probably stands for the crimson F. J. GROOTENDORST, a perpetual flowerer with small scentless blooms in clusters: height about 4 ft. PINK GROOTENDORST is a sport from it and claimed to be superior because the colours unite the foliage. Neither, I am afraid, has made much impression on me.

It is a great pity that ROSERAIE DE L'HAŸ is not more freely available. The purplish crimson flowers are very large and opulent. They come almost continuously and with much fragrance. In this respect they are unlike Parfum de l'Haÿ which is not all that perfumed and is generally undistinguished. Roseraie de l'Haÿ can get to 6 ft.

SPECIES ROSES : SWEET BRIARS : SCOTCH BRIARS

Under the headings, in many catalogues, of 'Species Roses'; 'Sweet Briars'; 'Scotch Briars' one will see some or all of the following shrub roses. They are all technically 'hybrids of the species', that is, of wild roses. For specimens of the species themselves one must normally go to the catalogues of a few specialist firms.

R. cantabrigiensis is a hybrid from two species, R. *hugonis* × R. *sericea*. As it grows to 7 ft., up and sideways, it is clearly better suited to the larger gardens. The long shoots are covered with fern-like leaves and, in May, with cream-yellow single flowers, many of which turn into small orange coloured heps. If room can be found it is well worthy of a place as a spring shrub. Incidentally R. *hugonis* itself has its followers.

Less space-demanding but equally early is the popularly named CANARY BIRD or more correctly **R. xanthina spontanea**. It has larger flowers than R. *cantabrigiensis*, which come somewhat earlier and are a rich (presumably canary) yellow. Truly the herald of the roses in spring: I have a fondness for it on that account and also because it was not too happy in my old thin-soiled garden, but transferred to the new one, where the conditions seem more suitable, is becoming quite a good bush (Plates 27 and 97).

R. moyesii is a wild rose from Western China and a big grower. The hybrids from it include the outstanding bright red GERANIUM which, while tall (up to 10 ft.), is more compact than the parent. The flowers — once a year only — are followed by very large heps.

R. rubiginosa is the 'Sweet Briar' and from it have been hybridized, amongst others, the Penzance group of Sweet Briar shrubs, noted for their display of heps as much as for their freely-given flowers and for their small leaved foliage, redolent of the sweet briar fragrance. Those most frequently offered are LORD PENZANCE, a fawn yellow; LADY PENZANCE, copper with a yellow centre; and MEG MERRILEES (which reaches 8 ft. compared with the Lord and Lady), a crimson. I have the last two and it is a real delight to enter

their area of fragrance as one goes along the shrub border. Unfortunately the Penzance group needs watching for black spot.

The species **R. spinosissima** is also known as the 'Burnett' or
'Scotch Briar'. The last mentioned ensures that the uninitiated confuse
it, as I did, with the Penzance group, which in addition to Meg
Merrilees includes two of Scott's other characters — Amy Robsart and
Julie Mannering. However, the important thing is that the ubiquitous
Wilhelm Kordes has obtained some magnificent hybrids with the
aid of *R. spinosissima*. Among them and readily obtainable are the
following:

FRÜHLINGSGOLD (Spring Gold), the sight of whose 7 ft. branches
weighed down, as it were, with 6 in. semi-double blooms along their
whole length, is one of the earliest joys of the rose season (Plates 29 and
97). The colour is a clear bright yellow, which goes towards white as
the flower ages. The fragrance from three bushes alongside each other
is outstanding. Such beauty is rightly not allowed to repeat itself in
the same year.

FRÜHLINGSMORGEN (Spring Morning) has deep pink single flowers
with yellow at the centre where the deeper toned stamens are prominent. Like Frühlingsgold it flowers in May, but unlike it, produces
some later blooms, but not many, followed by large maroon heps.
Not quite such a vigorous grower (Plate 97).

R. rubrifolia is sometimes offered. Its attractiveness comes mainly
from the red-brown bark and from the foliage in which that colour
overlays a greyish green. The flowers are a purplish pink and are
followed by dark red heps. It grows to 6 ft. and needs barbed wire
protection against the flower arrangers.

The 'AUSTRIAN COPPER' is unique in another way in that it has
provided all the flame, orange and bicoloured hybrid tea roses we
have. The insides of the petals are bright copper orange, while the
outside is yellow. They come once only. The name 'Austrian Copper'
is quite misleading: the correct one is **R. foetida bicolor.** It is a sport
from *R. foetida*, a wild rose of Western Asia and the Middle East, and
is not less than three hundred years old. Ultimate height said to be
about 5 ft., but it seems to get there rather slowly. Certainly worth
growing on its own account as well as for its historical value, which
includes the untrue allegation that it is the original source of black spot
in our modern roses.

NEVADA. A modern shrub (1927) frequently and rightly offered,
a pale creamy white (whose parentage is doubtful), which gives its

large flowers very freely indeed in May and early June and intermittently until another flush arrives early in August. Will go to about
7 ft. in both directions. Outstanding in the shrub border and as a
specimen on its own (Plate 28).

I do not think that anything more can be usefully said about the
shrub roses, within the limitation set, namely, that some or all of
the varieties discussed appear in the majority of rose nurserymen's
catalogues. But there are many, many more outstanding shrubs in the
catalogues of those who reckon to carry a fair stock in addition to
the ordinary kinds, and, more particularly, in the catalogues of the
few firms who specialize in the fields of shrub and old garden roses
or old French roses (as they are somewhat indefinitely called).

It is this limitation in the sources of supply which deters me from
discussing the Bourbons, Gallicas, Damasks, Albas, Centifolias and
China Roses. But who would not feel an urge to adventure into an
old world where common parlance includes such names as Maiden's
Blush, Celeste, Koenigen von Dänemark, Fantin la Tour, Chapeau de
Napoleon, Petite de Hollande, La Reine Victoria, Louise Odier,
Mme Ernst Calvat, Honorine de Brabant, Belle de Crécy, Cardinal
Richelieu and Rosa Mundi? There is glory for you. These and numerous other romantic and aromatic names are flowering before me
as I write. They have quite a different charm to that of the modern
roses, and for those who would like to savour it in their own gardens
may I commend Mr G. S. Thomas's *The Old Shrub Roses* and *The
Manual of Shrub Roses* compiled by him for the Sunningdale Nurseries.

IX

Standards, Collections and Miniature Roses

This chapter covers three quite unconnected subjects, but they complete the contents of the catalogues.

STANDARDS

Standard rose trees are simply the hybrid teas, floribundas and climbers budded onto a stock with a long stem instead of one with a short neck. At one time canina stock was *de rigueur* for the purpose, but it has been largely replaced by rugosa, which can easily be recognized by its prickly and rough skin. It is said to be less long lasting than canina, but so far I have not noticed it; admittedly my oldest rugosa standard is as yet only ten years old.

The ordinary standard is budded at about 3 ft. 6 in. up the stem. Half-standards budded at 2 ft. 6 in. are sometimes offered. Most of the very vigorous hybrid teas make good standards unless they are particularly upright growers. The less vigorous are inclined to produce 'mop heads'. Among the varieties discussed in Chapter V one can certainly rely, in my experience, upon Ena Harkness, Peace, Sultane, Eden Rose, Opera and Virgo. To these might be added two varieties which have with me justified their reputation of making better standards than bushes. They are the scarlet crimson New Yorker and Lydia, a bright golden yellow. Plate 42 shows Opera in the full form, and in good form too.

The vigorous growth of the floribundas makes them particularly suitable for standards. I have been particularly pleased with Frensham, Firecracker, Masquerade (Plate 95), Orangeade, Iceberg and Lilli Marlene (Plate 70), and Korona.

WEEPING STANDARDS used to be a great feature in more spacious

days: still obtainable, they are produced by budding wichuraiana
ramblers on rather taller stock than ordinarily used for standards.
My experience is limited to one only, Crimson Shower, which gives a
good display of small semi-double blooms of a not very pleasant
crimson over a longer period than most ramblers — something like
seven weeks. Others commonly met with are Dorothy Perkins,
Excelsa and Lady Godiva.

COLLECTIONS

Most catalogues offer at least two Collections, usually a dozen bushes
in each, one of hybrid teas and one of floribundas. Others carry more
and they often cover special features, such as the brightest colours,
the most fragrant, most shapely, and so on. Whatever the collection
it invariably shows a worthwhile reduction, usually between 12 per
cent and 15 per cent, on the catalogue price of the individual varieties.
If the contents of a particular collection happen to coincide with one's
wishes and one wants six or more of each variety the purchase of
half-a-dozen collections is a better buy than half-dozens at the dozen
rate, because the latter is usually 8 per cent below the price of individual bushes.

It should be noted, however, that quite naturally the nurserymen
reserve the right to alter the contents of the collections offered should
any variety become sold out, but in making these alterations many
undertake that the substitutes will be a more expensive variety. The
collections either as originally offered or with alterations will invariably be up to the standard of the grower: they are not a means of
getting rid of sub-standard stock.

In the make-up of these collections the nurserymen naturally show
their personal predilections as well as their judgement of popular
demand. In a sample of a dozen catalogues containing altogether 39
collections no two were the same. It is quite understandable, therefore,
when I say that for myself I have never been wholly satisfied with any
particular rose collection — not even with those where the nursery
men have faithfully followed the tables in the Annuals of the National
Rose Society showing how the experts have voted. Almost invariably
I am quite happy with ten or even eleven of the varieties but cannot
always understand why the other one or two are there. Here, however, as an illustration, is quite the best collection for a beginner which
I have seen offered among the hybrid teas:

Ena Harkness, Josephine Bruce, Eden Rose, Monique, Peace, Lady Belper, Spek's Yellow, Cleopatra, Sutter's Gold, Tzigane, Signora, Mme Butterfly.

A similar collection of floribundas which I think is hard to fault (except that the awkward height of Queen Elizabeth makes it difficult to put it in the same bed as the others) is:

Frensham, Korona, Jiminy Cricket, Circus, Masquerade, Allgold, Elsinore (or Moulin Rouge), Rosemary Rose, Sweet Repose, Firecracker, United Nations, Queen Elizabeth.

Although they do not appeal to me I recommend collections, especially for the beginner. They also make excellent presents which will be enjoyed, and the giver will be remembered long after more ephemeral gifts have been forgotten.

MINIATURES

Miniature roses have their charm and they are offered in quite a number of catalogues. I cannot say much about them from personal experience because my garden contains only six — all of the same variety. It may be useful, however, to point out that, although often sold in pots, they are not house plants in the usual meaning of that expression. They can be brought into the house for the flowering period, but as soon as that is over they ought to be taken out to a frame or greenhouse to grow on or they should be planted out and be treated like any other rose. They are true miniatures, growing from 6 to 12 in., and they have been bred from the China Roses.

X

Uses of the Various Kinds

One is inclined to be exceedingly brief here by saying — 'they are your roses, it is your garden, you and your family have to look at them, use them as you will'. Especially so, as gardens vary in size as much as do the ships on the seas. Moreover, personal tastes and pockets have an equally wide range. For instance, you may prefer to inter-mingle your roses with other flowers or you may incline to more orthodox ways by having them in separate beds or in a rose garden. If, however, this book is to be complete for those to whom it is addressed some explanation on the uses of the numerous types is necessary, especially in helping to get the best out of one's roses — few or many.

But before so doing, and having regard to the planting problems discussed in later chapters, it may be worth saying something about when our roses — in chief the hybrid teas and floribundas — may be expected to give their flowers.

FLOWERING PERIODS

One often sees the statement that roses bloom from May to December; something like it is said in this book. And so they can do, depending to some extent on the date of pruning (page 153)and to a much larger extent on the forwardness or otherwise of spring and similarly on the kind of autumn.

The growth of most plants in the British Isles begins, according to the experts, when the mean daily temperature exceeds 42°F., that is to say, 'spring' has arrived. In certain parts of the west and south-west coasts this mean is always present, so that there is no true rest from growth, and as regards the remainder of the country the average date of spring's arrival varies from mid-February in the extreme south to the fourth week in March in parts of Scotland; it arrives at the end of February in Lancashire and a week or more later on the north-east coast. The date is not, however, solely a question of latitude: such factors as the height above sea level, proximity to the sea, local shelter and the soil fertility and moisture bring about marked local variations.

The dates of the opening of the growing season mentioned above are said to be average dates. This means that one can have early or late springs, either generally or locally. My own measurement of this is taken from the date of my first rose blooms. Invariably they have come from Hugh Dickson, a real old timer, and Marcelle Gret, a Peace offspring, and from the climbing sports of Shot Silk and Mme Édouard Herriot. Taking Hugh Dickson as the measure one finds that the first blooms came in five years on June 2, May 30, May 4, May 31, and May 15. The record date of May 4 reflects the result of the phenomenally sunny spring of 1957.

The first blooms of a wide range of other varieties follow on those of Hugh Dickson over a period of three weeks. Among the earlier ones, in addition to Marcelle Gret, are Ena Harkness, Sutter's Gold, Picture, Golden Melody, McGredy's Yellow and Mrs Sam McGredy. Among newer roses Pink Favourite and Piccadilly were early too. An outstanding laggard, but so well worth waiting for, is Perfecta. In general, I find the floribundas are a week or so later than the hybrid teas. Leaders, by several lengths, in the early bloom stakes are invariably Frensham, the multi-coloured Salute and Korona.

We have seen that plant growth depends on the mean temperature remaining over 42°. The period over which this happens is the 'growing season', and it is somewhat surprising to learn that in this season there are as many growing days after July 31 as there are before — one has the rather vague idea that, come the end of October, all is over in the garden. Taking the mean date in my own locality — February 26 (after adjustment for height above sea level)—as an example, this mean that the growing season extends to Christmas. While this may be true as regards vegetation in general I have yet to pick rose blooms on Christmas Day. A worthwhile bowl of hybrid teas is, however, usually available at the end of November (Plate 107).

Taking one year and one thing with another I put my assured quality bloom season at about eighteen weeks running from first blooms at the beginning of June to the first week in October. During this period there will be two main flushes of bloom. The first will be pretty well at its best during the end of June and the first week or so of July. The other peak comes in the first half of September. This does not mean that one gets no roses in between. In the first place, as I have

Transferring roses: 58. A hole, about a foot square and a spade deep, prepared at new situation. Best done when soil in moist condition. 59. Tree to be removed loosened and finally freed from soil by four or more bold cuts about 10 in. from centre.

Transferring Roses: 60. Plant with ball of soil adhering carried apprehensively to new situation and — 61. eased into the prepared hole.

already mentioned, varieties vary between one another by as much as three weeks in coming into bloom, and secondly the flushes build up and die away gradually. There is also the important quality of freedom of flowering in which there is, as discussed in Chapter V, wide variation.

In the eighteen week period, 21 plants of Ena Harkness gave 460 blooms as follows:

in the first six weeks 180
in the succeeding six weeks 90
and in the remaining six weeks 190

During the same period 11 Picture gave a total of 330 blooms distributed as to 140:55:135. Nine bushes of Grand'mère Jenny produced their total of 220 in the sequence of 90:30:100.

These three are good examples of a number of varieties which give a pattern of the first and second flushes being almost equal while the intervening period produces between a half and a third of the flush output. Rose Gaujard and Sutter's Gold, of which there were a dozen of each, are examples of a different pattern, namely where there is a steady output in the first twelve weeks followed by an increased rate of production in the last six weeks. Sutter's Gold showed 60:60:120 and Rose Gaujard 70:65:90.

The position with regard to the floribundas is, of course, rather different. The number of blooms is no real measure even if counting were a practical proposition. The alternative test seems to be whether there are extensive periods between one flush and another. Unlike the hybrid teas, which never seem to be quite out of bloom, some floribundas have flowerless periods. There are, however, notable exceptions such as Korona and Frensham. It is a field open to research.

HYBRID TEAS AND FLORIBUNDAS

Whatever may be the precise meaning of 'bedding rose' as applied to hybrid teas (page 37) it may be taken that 'bedding' is the operative word and that the hybrid teas are best grown in beds; and by beds one means beds and not borders in that the former allows the rose to be seen and enjoyed from all angles.

The floribundas are, of course, the 'bedding rose' par excellence. They can provide vivid and long lasting splashes of colour where it may be most needed, whether near the house in the small garden or massed in the distance in the larger one. Since, however, the examination of the individual blooms or trusses is not usually one of the

joys one gets from the floribundas, they are equally suitable for a border, where advantage can be taken of their wide range of height, for
example, the tall growing Queen Elizabeth at the back, with the
shorter Allgold in the front row.

It has been mentioned that one may be inclined to put roses among
other flowers; for example, in the herbaceous border. By all means
do so if you wish, but I think you will find that certainly the hybrid
teas will not give you much satisfaction there, whether in a group or
as individual plants. Somehow they are the wrong shape both of
flower and bush to fit in happily with other bedding and border
plants. One gets much the same feeling with the floribundas, too. And
as regards both types the colours, especially the vivid ones, do not
seem to fit the general tone. Some people, however, find that the
softer tones of the old garden roses and those of the hybrid musks
can be fitted agreeably into the herbaceous border. I have no such
border, but in Chapter XIII a mixed border is briefly described which
makes use, I believe successfully, of climbers, shrub roses, old garden
roses and floribundas with other plants, in a very restricted range.

Some of the more vigorously growing hybrid teas and floribundas
lend themselves to treatment as INDIVIDUAL SHRUBS when lightly
pruned (page 151). Peace is a notable example: others among the
hybrid teas are Eden Rose, Grand Gala, Rose Gaujard and Grand'mère
Jenny. Hector Deane, salmon-carmine, is another and has the added
attraction of its fragrance. Hugh Dickson and Frau Karl Druschki (not
strictly hybrid teas but of that type) do well if their shoots are pegged
down at ground level. Among the floribundas making good shrub-
like growth are Queen Elizabeth, Frensham and Ama. Dainty Maid
can be good too. The Spartan in Plate 30 was not grown specially as an
individual bush, but it developed well and has been encouraged by
moderate and light-pruning to built up gradually to 6 ft. — this is the
best way to make these shrubs.

STANDARDS

My earliest rose recollection is of the standards which flanked the
short path from the gate to the front door of our pre-1914 seaside
home. I do not remember their colours, but I do recall spraying them
with, I believe, soapy water against the greenfly. Standards are still
used as path flankers and, no doubt, give satisfaction when so used,
but they are perhaps to be preferred as 'line-breakers' among the bush
roses where uniformity of height can be monotonous, especially in

Transferring Roses: 62. Some planting mixture is used to fill in spaces and cracks. 63. Plant firmed in and all foliage is removed — the author usually combines pruning with this operation.

When planting out in spring, pruning is done before planting. 64. (Above, left) Bush with roots trimmed to 8–10 in. ready for pruning.

65. (Above) Cut made to an outward pointing eye about 6 in. from union; slope of cut follows direction of the eye. The cut about to be made is incorrect — the secateurs should be pointing down, not up.

66. Pruning completed and the bush ready for planting.

large beds. Here they can be very effective either at the ends or at intervals.

What cannot be recommended is standards set in the lawn in
round holes — presumably to break its monotony, but surely the
beauty of a calm sea or a desert is its monotony? Keeping the weeds
down, cutting the circular edge of the grass and getting dizzy when
mowing all seem to add up to unworthwhile labour. I have made
the round-hole-in-the-lawn mistake, and my son, who has mowed my
grass in holidays and vacations for many years, has strong views about
this aspect of garden layout. If, despite the warning, one has an
irrepressible urge for standards in the lawn, pray make the hole at
least 3 ft. in diameter, otherwise even the most vigorous variety will
be mop headed.

Those who have used ramblers to cover wooden fences will have
suffered from the labour of untying, pruning and re-tying, to say
nothing of the annoyance to the neighbours who do not like ramblers.
Standards can achieve the same effect as the ramblers much more
pleasantly and with a fraction of the labour requirements of the
ramblers. In this connection, however, I recall a remark of Mrs
Margery Fish — an outstanding garden maker — that labour saving
in the garden, as elsewhere, invariably entails spending money in
some other way: in this present instance the standards or half-standards
required to cover the top of a given length of fencing will certainly
cost more than ramblers would do. Normally, however, they will do
the job quicker.

CLIMBERS

If it is felt that the RAMBLERS are not worth the work and irritation
involved when grown on pillars, arches and fences (they should never
be used on walls owing to their predisposition to mildew), how are
they to be used? One way has been mentioned when discussing Albertine: namely, to let them ramble on their own up trees, and this idea
can obviously be extended to old tree stumps and to hedges. But need
they be up in the air? They will ramble equally well on ground where
they will give excellent cover to grassy slopes or to banks or in the
difficult bed where owing to trees or other causes nothing seems to do
well. I am using them in this way to hide the concrete cover of a
septic tank. My word will have to be taken that the variety used was
selected by chance and not by design: it is a pure white, called Purity.

G

Among the LARGE FLOWERED CLIMBERS, the sports of the hybrid teas are often recommended for growing on walls. The need for fanlike and horizontal training, however, entails constant provision of nails or staples with the accompanying tying up with twine or wire which the use of trellis against the house will not avoid. But those of us who seek a worthwhile garden entirely without labour are seeking for — I was going to say the moon — the impossible. It may be that I am prejudiced owing to the poor results over a good many years which I had with climbing Étoile de Hollande, Lady Sylvia and Golden Dawn on a south-west wall, but I prefer to grow them on wire fences or pillars.

On the other hand some climbers mentioned in Chapter VII do well on walls, Danse du Feu is said to do very well on any wall — north, south, east or west — while Elegance is offered for the south or west sides only. Mermaid is outstanding on a wall provided one is prepared to be patient (see page 79). What I have said about climbers on walls does not prevent me from enjoining on those people whose houses support old and flourishing climbers such as Mme Alfred Carrière, Mme Abel Chatenay and, of course, old Gloire de Dijon, to give them all the care and attention that the aged and the beautiful deserve.

It will be noticed in Plate 24 that the stems of the climbing sport illustrated do not go straight up, but are fan-trained and run out on horizontal wires at various heights. This is by far the best way as these sports are vigorous, but need to be checked in order to get the maximum yield of bloom. If they are required as a pillar then the stems should be twisted round the pole and tied. While they will be satisfactory grown in that way, the horizontal training is much the better.

PILLAR ROSES describe their own use and they are equally good on arches and on pergolas. A stoutly built arch with the posts in concrete can be an agreeable entrance from one part of the garden to another, but it hardly does for a pergola, which for permanence requires brick pillars, heavy timbers and hence a long pocket. This is a pity because a well designed and well constructed pergola can be an excellent feature in the right garden, particularly if clematis are grown among the roses.

As regards pillars, however, I commend them, as a less expensive alternative to standards, as line breakers in the beds of hybrid teas and floribundas. Danse du Feu and three other large Flowered Climbers not previously mentioned, Parade (carmine crimson), Coral Dawn (pink), and Aloha (deep rose pink), were effectively so used in my previous garden as well as the climbing sports. The Kordesii climbers are obvious material for use in this way.

Instead of using single pillars three can be put tripod fashion, with a climber trained up each leg. A labour saving device I am now using is to let the climbers grow up inside the tripod, simply supported by the horizontal braces over which they flow. The informal result is a pleasant change and looks well in a large bed of shrub roses.

SCREENS AND HEDGES

It may have been gathered that climbing roses, in variety, have been used as a tall boundary screen or hedge in my garden. In three growing seasons it appears to have made pretty good progress — it appears in a number of plates — but the climbers have been put in pretty thickly, nearly 90 in 100 yds. In the summer, in addition to great beauty, it fulfils its function admirably, but it fails completely when the leaves have fallen. Nevertheless, it is well worth while until it can be replaced in some parts and fortified in others with tall thick growing shrubs.

The winter lack of opacity is, unfortunately, a common weakness of rose hedges, no matter what varieties are used. But for many people the summer beauty provides more than adequate compensation. The shrub roses can be used for hedges and they will give 5 ft. or more in height. The modern hybrid musk, Bonn, has been used as a screening hedge round the previously mentioned septic tank. I have seen two of the newer shrubs, Heidelburg and Munster, making tall and effective hedges and I have used Zéphirine Drouhin, trained on wires, to give a 4 ft. high screen.

The taller growing floribundas can also be used with good effect if planted not more than 2 ft. apart. I can recommend Frensham as providing both beauty and barbed wire. Masquerade and Dainty Maid are two of the tall growers which can be used, but close planting is essential. For hedges up to about 4 ft. the hybrid musks are said to be very good and can be kept cut back with garden shears rather than by orthodox pruning, but care in selection of varieties is necessary to ensure uniformity of height.

XI

Rose Beds and how to fill them

THIS chapter continues the theme of the previous one in trying to
help in making the best use of one's roses and setting them off to the
best advantage — as individual plants and, particularly, in larger
units.

Those with established gardens will, no doubt, have at least one rose
bed and may feel that it is fixed for all time; others may be thinking of extending their use of roses as an economy of money, time and
labour. I hope that what is said in Chapter XV will show that making
new rose beds is not quite such a major operation as one may think.
Then there are the thousands of people going into brand new houses
with every aid and convenience that modern skill and design provide
but which leaves the age-old problem just as it was — the garden
which has to be started from scratch. And even when it does not have
to be dug it usually has to be designed and filled. Those of us so situated, however, do have the opportunity of working, as it were, on a
clean canvas, but, if I am a fair sample, it will not prevent us making
mistakes.

SITUATION OF BEDS

Sergeant Cuff had something when he said 'Ah, you've got the right
exposure here to south and south-west.' But all of us cannot have this
ideal siting for our roses. It is nevertheless worth keeping in mind
and we can at least avoid putting our rose beds in a sunless north aspect,
unless it be climbers which are noted for use on 'north walls'.

We would be wise to avoid the vicinity of large trees. It is not
always realized that the root system of a tree is certainly not less in
diameter than that of the area covered by the foliage system. If then in
digging a bed in the neighbourhood of a tree one finds roots, take it as
a warning. Peace can hardly be described as other than very vigorous
and they were very much so in my old garden. In the new one they

67. *Gail Borden — a lovely rose. What other 'lovelies' would look like this after standing in the rain for over six hours? Beauty of this kind does not come abundantly.*

68. *The floribundas can be beautiful too: the cherry red Elsinore with Ivory Fashion and Jiminy Cricket. Picture taken late September when Ivory Fashion is at its best.*

were put in a bed only 18 ft. south of the trunks of the large trees shown in the background of Plate 31. In two years they never moved and gave very few blooms: they had to be shifted.

Hedges are very hungry vegetation, especially privet, so keep roses well away from them lest they poach the food provided for the roses. On the same line of thought remember too that the eaves and gutters make the soil particularly dry near the walls of the house so if one thinks it is worth using climbers there be sure to plant them *at least* 18 in. out from the walls and during dry weather give each climber at least 3 gallons of water a week.

SIZE, SHAPE AND SURROUNDINGS OF BEDS

The orthodox ideas for rose beds are rectangles not more than 6 ft. wide, or shapes making up a pattern, for example, like that in Plate 34. Such ideas have persisted for many years. For instance Sergeant Cuff would have it that there was 'nothing like a circle set in a square . . . with walks in between the beds'.

The idea of beds not exceeding 6 ft. in width is for ease of 'cultivation', which means, I take it, that one can prune, dig over, fertilize, weed, spray, cut off the dead heads and so on without treading on the beds. Some of these operations can be thus done, but I for one cannot do them all. Anyway pricking out a few footmarks is not exactly a laborious job. And the footmarks will indeed be faint if the beds are adequately mulched (page 170). Perhaps the 6 ft. idea is one of those pieces of gardening lore which needs to be observed a little more in the breach. Make your beds bigger if it suits you and the design of your garden as I have done under expert advice, with I hope very good effect too.

On the other hand, I go a very long way indeed with those people who hold with Sergeant Cuff that the walks between the beds should be 'grass, Mr Gardener — grass walks between your roses; gravel's too hard for them'. And with 'gravel' I take it that the Sergeant would include paving of all kinds and bricks too. Well kept grass cannot be surpassed for showing off one's hybrid teas and floribundas, notwithstanding its demand for neatly trimmed edges. But grass is not always convenient or possible. I have in mind the small garden in inner London or an industrial town where grass is difficult to grow or to keep well or where size does not warrant the paraphernalia of lawnmower and edging tools. Here stone or brick is better than grass.

Plates 32 to 34 illustrate such a rose garden, 30 ft. square, where Miss Sylvia Crowe, P.P.I.L.A., has made use of local Sussex bricks to produce a small rose and shrub garden, not only complete in itself but as an integral part of a much larger scheme.

But to return to our grass setting for rose beds: there is no doubt that long 6 ft. wide beds facilitate long uninterrupted cuts with the mower and it was pre-occupation with this idea which led me into the mistake I made in the design of my main rose garden (of this later). Actually 'fish-shaped' beds can assist in uninterrupted mowing just as well if not better than the straight up and down beds, and they have the added advantage of avoiding a regimented appearance. But such beds do not seem able to cope with roses very well when more than one variety has to be used.

ARRANGEMENT WITHIN THE BEDS

There is a school of thought which favours having beds of one variety. By all means do this if you have the means, but I am pretty sure that 75 per cent of roses — hybrid teas and floribundas — are in mixed beds. After all a dozen roses need no more than a bed 8 ft. by 6 ft. which can hardly be described as large, and most people will want something bigger. But even if the dozen basis be accepted it severely restricts one's choice of varieties, as a hundred roses so divided will cover only eight or nine varieties. On the other hand, if the beds are made big enough to take a couple of dozen, 240 will be needed to provide ten varieties. Most people would wish to get a more extensive knowledge of roses than these arrangements provide.

At the other end of the scale there is 'one of each variety'. My experience suggests that, although this may be acceptable for a first step in rose growing, it will not satisfy one for long. First, because the varying colours tend to give a spotty effect in the garden and, second, the performance of one plant is hardly a fair test of a particular variety. For such a purpose the National Rose Society ask for six in their Trial Ground and I am bound to say that on all counts I would prefer not to have less than that number, although for many years I had to be content with three of each.

Whether one has one, three, six, or more, the usual planting distance apart of the hybrid teas is 18 to 24 in. depending on the vigour of the variety. More than 24 in. will usually be found too much except for the very vigorous growers like Peace, when 30 in. should be given. (I once put 15 bushes of this variety in a bed 8 ft. × 6 ft. and thereafter wondered why they were such black spot addicts). In general the floribundas will do best at not less than 24 in. and, usually, except for the shorter kinds, 30 in. is better — certainly not less than that for Frensham and its like.

Whatever the number of each variety and whatever the distance apart, the orthodox 6 ft. wide bed will normally impose a pattern of planting either like this:

```
    X       X   :   X       X   :   X       X
A   X       X   :   X       X   :   X       X
    X       X   :   X       X   :   X       X
```

or, like this:

```
    X       X  ···. X       X  ···. X       X
B     X       X   X     X       X   X       X
    X       X  ···  X       X  ···  X       X
```

Ena Harkness   McGredy's Yellow   Opera

The staggered formation of B certainly looks more attractive as a pattern, but it does entail a kind of overlap at the point where one variety ends and another begins. The dotted lines show how this comes with six of each variety, but it is, of course, the same whatever the number may be above three. This pattern may also produce problems of height and other difficulties which may worry some people, although they ought not to be taken too seriously. They did not worry me and I used pattern B for many years.

In the new garden A was adopted and I well remember a visitor walking round the beds in early spring, saying: 'But you are not going to leave them in rows like that?' I quite understood what he was getting at — regularity was being carried too far and the effect was like a nursery. With the bushes fully foliaged, however, I am quite sure that in the ordinary way no one is aware of how the plants are arranged. The important thing about pattern A is that it allows straight runs with the hoe whereas in pattern B the hoe is impeded by the plants in the intervening middle row. A sharp hoe, especially if one is getting a little tired and therefore careless, can do some nasty damage. A long tale about very little? Perhaps, but such a 'very little' of this kind can make quite a difference to the work one has to put into the rose beds.

With square and small rectangular beds there is infinite variety of triangular and other patterns available for planting out the rose bushes. They depend on one's taste and ingenuity. But keep the need for easy hoeing in mind. There is, too, that circular bed mentioned by Sergeant Cuff, but I have never had the courage to cope with more than one variety in such a bed.

Whatever the shape of the bed you are, of course, going to grow fine and vigorous roses. If they extend too much over the edge of the grass there is a real likelihood that they will be damaged by the mower, to say nothing of the bloody wounds on one's hands from the armature of the roses. Take care, therefore, to plant 18 in. from the grass edge: 1 ft. is not enough.

VARIATIONS IN HEIGHT

Having looked at the horizontal, what of the vertical? One of the points urged in favour of having one variety only in each bed is that it secures uniformity of height. *Per contra*, as varieties vary in height, a mixed bed is wrong or the result is unhappy if tall growers come alongside shorter ones and so on. I do not see it that way. The need to break the monotony to the eye has already been mentioned in relation to the uses of standards and pillar roses. If the bush roses can do the job themselves, why not allow them to do so? Of course, there must be reason in all things. One would hardly put the somewhat below average Concerto next to the tall growing Faust, but it could be followed quite well by Iceberg, Red Favourite and Rosemary Rose. And I am not in the least worried by Chrysler Imperial being flanked by the tall growing Eden Rose and Monique, but Cleopatra next to Grace de Monaco is going too far. In these illustrations, however, I have not consciously taken into account the effects of the different colours, the problems of which are canvassed in the next chapter.

XII

The Problems of Colour and of Under-planting

Colour schemes can be controversial to a degree; perhaps because it is much more of a woman's problem than a man's. However, whatever may happen inside the house, in the garden the man will, at least, have to assist in the solution, if only by timely praise of his wife's cleverness in showing where he has gone wrong. Sergeant Cuff was unmarried so he had the free exercise of his own taste. His ' . . . white roses and blush roses. They always mix well together, don't they?' may be a glimpse of the obvious, but it does reflect his realization that mixing roses can give added appreciation and enjoyment.

MIXING COLOURS

One of the many mistakes I have made in my rose growing, and one which still brings a flush of shame and annoyance, was when I replaced, as so many people do, a herbaceous border with a large bed of hybrid tea roses. I bought a dozen each of four varieties and, un-advised and unread, I decided that the colours would look less mono-tonous if they were well mixed.

This I proceeded to do by laying out on the lawn one each of Lady Sylvia, Mme Jules Bouché, Caroline Testout, Crimson Glory, and then repeating. Of course each bush was not separately labelled and I soon forgot the order I was using. The result was quite dreadful. Ever since I have been at great pains to keep each variety to itself whether it be three in number or two dozen. Later on, as experience came, I realised that the beauty of many varieties could be much en-hanced by taking more care in the selection of their neighbours and that, had my first efforts been confined to two varieties and not to four, it might not have been a mistake at all.

As so often happens this realization came quite fortuitously. First,

I was suddenly struck by the particular beauty produced in one of my own beds by the deep orange and flame red of Mojave alongside the brilliant tone of Spek's Yellow. Then, when visiting a nursery, I saw how a row of rather dull red floribundas was enhanced by the next row of a new golden yellow.

Broadly there are two ways of pairing varieties. One is to interplant them: there are a number of ways of doing this, e.g., alternately or have blocks of the varieties alongside each other.

What follows are some suggestions which I have already tried. But colour is so much a matter of individual taste that it is really best worked out to one's own ideas, not forgetting foliage and height of growth. These ideas are not only for the larger grower; I am quite sure that anyone contemplating a first purchase of half-a-dozen floribundas will get, for example, more beauty and satisfaction from an interplanting of three orange-scarlet Korona with three Allgold in front, rather than from six of the same variety.

Quite by chance, the bed which contains the Mojave and the Spek's Yellow provides a good illustration of what is in mind. It contains Christian Dior, crimson: Virgo, white; Ena Harkness, crimson-scarlet; Spek's Yellow; Mojave, orange-flame; and La Jolla, in pastel pink shades. Each enhances or is enhanced by its neighbour or neighbours. I hope, however, that the superstition about not having red and white roses in the same bowl does not extend to rose beds.

The pink flowers of Picture with those of McGredy's Yellow can be a happy use of pinks and yellows, Plate 37. As an example of interplanting of the tall-growing hybrid tea type of floribunda, I have had groups of three Queen Elizabeths separated by single plants of the yellow Buccaneer (usually described as a hybrid tea), but excellent alternatives would be the bright yellow Faust or Spek's Yellow.

Among the floribundas, I have already mentioned Allgold and Korona. These have been interplanted and, although Korona is the taller grower, it seems to work very well. The People makes a good substitute for Korona (Plate 94). Others recommended for interplanting are the kaleidoscopic Masquerade with the crimson Alain.

The white Iceberg and Orangeade are a natural and cooling combination. Among low growers Meteor, orange, alongside Rodeo, scarlet, has somewhat unexpectedly looked very nice. Last but by no means least are two old-timers — the pink Dainty Maid with the almost black-red Dusky Maiden in front. Be sure, however, to dead-head Dusky Maiden as soon as the flowers are over.

Examples of the pillar climbers which I have paired are the red New Blaze with the new Golden Showers; orange-scarlet Bonn with deep yellow High Noon — I regard this combination as particularly good — and Goldilocks with Danse du Feu, another orange-scarlet. Incidentally, all these climbers are 'perpetuals'.

Now this kind of thing may be all very well when one has lots of roses and lots of colours to play around with, but if, for instance, one is making a beginning with a mixed dozen of the hybrid teas mentioned in Chapter V, what about them? How could they be arranged with regard to colours in a small conventional bed?

Well, I think, with diffidence, that a selection laid out as below might give greater pleasure than if it were put in at random.

Eden Rose	Perfecta	Ena Harkness	Peace
(*deep rose pink*)	(*cream and rose pink*)	(*crimson-scarlet*)	(*yellow shaded pink at edges*)
Spek's Yellow	Konrad Adenauer	Opera	McGredy's Yellow
	(*crimson*)	(*orange-red*)	
Josephine Bruce	Margaret	Mrs Sam McGredy	Mme Louis Laperrière
(*crimson-scarlet*)	(*bright pink*)	(*coppery pink*)	(*dark crimson*)

As regards the collection shown on page 89, this might be planted:

Eden Rose	Mme Butterfly	Ena Harkness	Peace
(*deep rose pink*)	(*salmon-flesh*)	(*crimson-scarlet*)	(*yellow, shaded pink at edges*)
Spek's Yellow	Josephine Bruce	Signora	Sutter's Gold
	(*crimson-scarlet*)	(*orange red/pink*)	(*light yellow, flushed indian red*)
Tzigane	Monique	Lady Belper	Cleopatra
(*bicolour red-yellow*)	(*silvery pink*)	(*light orange-yellow*)	(*bicolour scarlet and golden yellow*)

The collection of floribundas might be put:

Queen Elizabeth	Frensham	Masquerade	Elsinore
(*pink*)	(*scarlet-crimson*)	(*yellow-pink-red*)	(*cherry red*)
Firecracker	United Nations	Korona	Jiminy Cricket
(*deep orange-pink*)	(*light pink*)	(*bright orange-scarlet*)	(*salmon-carmine*)
Circus	Rosemary Rose	Allgold	Sweet Repose
(*yellow flushed pink*)	(*bright carmine*)	(*deepish yellow*)	(*light pink*)

These suggestions may be quite unacceptable to some people, others may improve upon them, while yet others would say that the given colours can in no way be reconciled harmoniously. Personal taste, thank goodness, is really the final arbiter. What I have said about roses cheek to cheek and the suggestions above may help to stimulate it.

By the way, what most people do seem to agree upon is that beds of *one colour* as opposed to beds of *one variety* are not a good thing: indeed, the very opposite.

OTHER PLANTS WITH ROSES

The purists insist that modern roses should be left entirely to themselves in the severity of formal beds. It is claimed that in this way they show themselves to the best advantage. As one who can get aesthetic pleasure from such a bed of newly pruned roses, with its pattern of cut stems against a clear sky or against the clean brown soil and from the wonderful variation in the colours and tones of the foliage as it appears in the spring (Plate 106), I have sympathy with this point of view. But those who do not see things in quite this way may well wish to have more than coloured foliage in the rose beds in the spring. Indeed they may feel that until the rose beds are pruned they look pretty tatty and, as regards the summer, the more the plants, the fewer the weeds. Why should they not? As I have said before it is their garden. And who wants to be a purist anyway?

Those that feel this way will carpet their rose beds with arabis, alyssum and aubrieta for spring display, with daffodils and polyanthus to follow. For the summer there will be, in their turn, pinks, violas, and dwarf annuals such as blue ageratum, lobelia and candytuft. Thyme also has its adherents.

It is no good for those who think otherwise to urge that roses dislike other plants and their quality will suffer, because it is not really true. But carpeting of this kind may make the feeding of the roses an awkward operation and the fertilizer may make the underplants too vigorous. Those gardeners who dislike 'hand-and-knees' work will eschew the annuals because of the thinning out involved, and it is no use thinking that the carpet will keep out all the weeds. It may also be well to remember that the polyanthus must be removed to other quarters after flowering and that roses have thorns.

EDGING AS A COMPROMISE

More cautiously-minded people may feel that at least the edges of the beds can be embellished with pinks (as much as for the contrasting light grey foliage as for the flowers), and small bulb flowers like the muscari and species crocus. They may also think that arabis can be used here. If, however, they want their rose beds among grass they will remember how irritating and work-making the introduction of edging plants can be. Here again personal taste and circumstances must decide.

69. *Chanelle (lower left) and Concerto (left) a bright scarlet. Circus comes next. Red Favourite is deeper scarlet crimson than shown.*
70. *Lilli Marlene (left) has a lovely velvety sheen. Orangeade (right) is aptly named. Iceberg is a long awaited good white.*

71. *Blooms, not trusses, of (from top) — United Nations, pink with yellow centres and two popular sellers, Firecracker, carmine shading to yellow, and Sweet Repose varying on light yellow and pink.*

72. *Dainty Maid is well named and remains so in any weather.*

XIII

Rose Gardens and a Mixed Border

It may be thought that in the small formal rose and shrub garden shown in Plates 32 to 34, and the plans on pages 112 and 113, and in the mixed border described later, a form of compromise has been achieved, under expert guidance, in a solution of the under-planting and edging problems discussed in the previous chapter. No compromise satisfies everybody: but here the formal garden avoids, with the use of shrubs, the winter starkness of the rose beds, provides interesting contrasting foliage and a succession of colour tones from spring to late autumn. The brick paths require no work at all (a yearly dose of sodium chlorate will take care of any weeds).

In detail it is composed as follows:

West side. Carried on the western red cedar screen are the perpetual climbers Danse du Feu and Leverküsen, with the tall growing shrub roses Elmshorn and Berlin in between. In front of them are irises, whose spiky foliage provides a pleasant contrast to that of the roses and as they increase in height will help to cover flowerless lower stems. For added interest mixed varieties of modern bearded iris are favoured including such well known varieties as New Snow (white), Bellerine (crimson), Copper River (brown), Andalusian (blue), Jane Phillips (blue), Chivalry (mid-blue), and Pink Cameo.

Among the irises are some choice daffodils and an edging, common also to the rose beds, is provided by dwarf Dutch lavender.

North and South sides. Both contain *Cotoneaster franchetii*, but the north west corner has in addition *C. frigida* beneath a *Malus floribunda*.

East side. (Against west wall of the house). This contains all the hybrid musk roses mentioned in Chapter VIII, treated as bedding roses. Also there are a pittosporum, *Viburnum davidii* and caryopteris. This side is edged with Allwoodii pinks and auriculas.

Rose Beds. These are, as already mentioned, edged with lavender and contain at present new hybrid teas the performance of which it is desired to watch handily from the house. They will be replaced with a permanent planting of the smaller growing floribundas such as Meteor, Rumba, Concerto, Allgold and Rodeo. The beds are mulched with peat moss.

One can imagine such a simple rose-cum-shrub and flower garden giving much pleasure to a person who cannot be too active or to the person with little time for gardening. Its size of 30 ft. square is governed by the space it was set out to fill — some proportionate enlargement could be made, but it should certainly not be much. As it stands Miss Sylvia Crowe has achieved, so far as I am concerned, what was asked — a rose garden involving minimum labour with maximum all-the-year-round interest. The cost of making this garden is given in Chapter XXI.

This rather pocket-handkerchief rose garden is not only complete in itself, but it serves to link the house to the garden generally. Plate 31 shows how necessary this was. At the same time it merges into a wider scheme, part of which is the very large bed of floribundas, fronted by plants of rosemary and to be fortified at the back with *Elaeagnus macrophylla*, *Sorbaria arborea* and *Ligustrum japonicum*.

The border then sweeps out to carry *Cotoneaster lactea* and *Viburnum tomentosum*. The Lily pond with its bordering plants is a feature and is linked to the sweeping border by a bed of *Rosa macrantha* bordered by more *Cotoneaster franchetii*. With the four fruit trees on the east side the design together with the house covers an area of about 200 ft. by 80 ft. — a not unusual size for a family house.

DANGERS OF COPYING

By illustrating two gardens mainly composed of roses it can be suggested that I am inviting people to copy them. The small formal garden in the size given might be happily reproduced in another setting; the larger plan, however, needs a much more cautious approach as, with respect, do most illustrative garden plans. Site, position of house, levels, aspect, to say nothing of personal predilections leading to modifications which may upset the whole balance of a design, are most important. I illustrate this with a cautionary tale.

Plate 35 shows my present main rose garden. The beds are either 45 or 48 ft. in length (roughly 84 roses in each). At the far end is a rose shrubbery. The grass rides or paths between the beds vary in width in an attempt to break regularity. It will be obvious from the plate that the east to west beds present an unbroken wall — although the height has been varied by the use of standards. This solid wall gives no vista through to the shrubbery and the field beyond, nor is any lead given to the eye to travel on to the South Downs. Moreover, the effect of the eastern border of floribundas and the fence of climbing sports is to divide an already rather narrow site and so make it appear even narrower. The contents of the beds may be beautiful but their layout is unfortunate — especially as one seeks a garden and not a display ground.

Now this design was taken from a book. It represented the adaptation of a tennis court to a rose garden with the proportions that such a site arbitrarily imposes. Moreover, one of its long sides lay immediately under the terrace of the house and the sloping bank to this gave an added interest. To take this design, site it over 60 ft. from the house on sloping ground, change its direction and increase the length of the beds by 50 per cent, is to make the worst possible use of a design, which was admirably suited to its own particular surroundings and purpose.

The impatience of youth is equalled by that of the not so young. Resist the temptation to copy blindly someone else's plan whether in altering an existing garden or for a new site. As to the latter it may be well to seek expert advice, but failing this go into residence for some while and so get the feel of the house and its surroundings, before attempting to make the garden.

One other and most important tip — whether the garden be large or small, a rose or a general garden — pay particular attention to the view from the window above the kitchen sink.

A MIXED BORDER

Whatever the design of the garden there is usually a border, so I am less cautious about giving particulars of a labour-saving border which, based mainly on roses of all kinds, makes use of some other flowers. It also gives, I believe, an example of how selected floribundas can be happily used in succession to the once-flowering old garden and shrub roses, whose graceful arching stems, together with a hedge of climbers provide a solid and varied background to the continuous flowering floribunda. This border faces south-east and I here describe some 40 ft. of it as being a likely convenient size for an average garden. The width is about 8 ft.

The background climbers are planted against poles at 6 ft. intervals and then trained along wires. They are, however, used somewhat

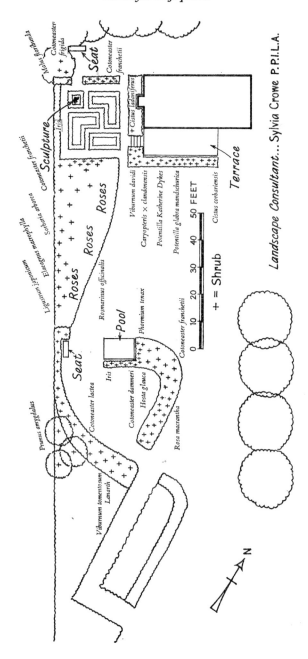

Cotoneaster frigida
Cotoneaster franchetii
Malus floribunda
Seat
Seat
Sculpture
Iris
Cistus ladaniferus
Cotoneaster franchetii
Sorbaria arborea
Elaeagnus macrophylla
Ligustrum japonicum
Roses Roses
Roses Roses
Viburnum davidi
Caryopteris × clandonensis
Potentilla Katherine Dykes
Potentilla glabra mandschurica
Terrace
Cistus corbariensis
Rosmarinus officinalis
Pool
Phormium tenax
Seat
Iris
Cotoneaster lactea
Cotoneaster dammeri
Hosta glauca
Rosa macrantha
Cotoneaster franchetii
Prunus amygdalus
Viburnum tomentosum / Lanarth

0 10 20 30 40 50 FEET
+ = Shrub

N

Landscape Consultant...Sylvia Crowe P.P.I.L.A.

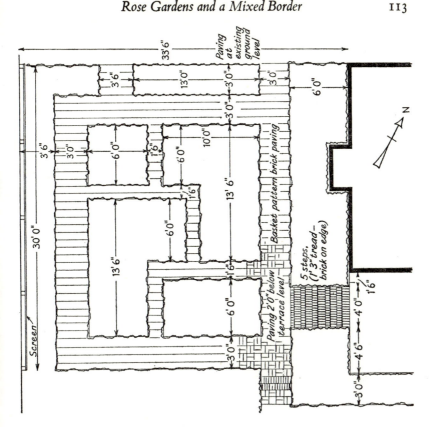

Plan of the rose and shrub gardens designed by Miss Sylvia Crowe for part of the author's garden. By the house is the Sister Anne rose garden (detailed plan opposite), which is complete in itself but also merges into the wider scheme. The bed on the left of the plan (above) is for roses and its direction is to bring one's eye to the South Downs: the pattern is repeated in further beds.

extravagantly to the extent that a once-flowering variety will have a continuous variety planted with it so as to ensure long periods of bloom. The climbers used include the New Dawn, Albertine, Emily Gray, Climbing Goldilocks and Golden Shower from those already described in Chapter VIII. In addition there are the rosy-crimson Excelsa, Meg, an apricot yellow, the fragrant Sander's White, Parade, a rosy-red, and the deep pink Aloha.

The shrub roses used are Schneezwerg (white), Roseraie de l'Haÿ (purple), Blanc Double de Coubert (white), and Conrad F. Meyer (silvery pink) — all rugosas, while the gallicas have provided Cardinal Richelieu, in maroon, Charles de Mills in crimson-purple and the shorter Georges Vibert in striped crimson. Great Maiden's Blush, an alba, has a place, but one somewhat removed from the species and their near varieties. The latter include *R. forrestiana*, a pink from western China, which makes an abundant contribution to the massed foliage as well as providing excellent heps. *R. rubrifolia* gives many heps too, as well as the pleasing contrast of its grey-green foliage. Then there are the groupings of the outstandingly beautiful Frühlingsgold and Frühlingsmorgen.

Interspersed with these, in the main, tall-growing shrubs are foxgloves for the early summer and the taller growing michaelmas daisies for the late season.

In front come the floribundas in groups of three. They include Masquerade, Dickson's Flame, Flamenco, Vogue, August Seebauer, Lilli Marlene, Chanelle, Yellow Hammer, Orange Sensation and Tambourine. The idea is that the shrubs, which are chiefly summer flowering only, will be practically over before the floribundas take over. Actually there is something of an overlap and for this reason I should be disposed in any re-arrangement to exclude the 'hotter' coloured floribundas in favour of more of the creams, yellows and softer pinks to which the shrubs and the old roses take more kindly.

Between the floribundas are groups of iris, while the really early spring colour comes from daffodils in which the white varieties figure.

Let us be clear: such a border is not going to be a perpetual blaze of glory. It will, however, for many months — over six in the south — have colour in it of some kind or another, and, subject to the modification I have mentioned, these colours will be a soothing contrast to the vividness of adjacent rose beds.

The end piece of this chapter is the same as the opening of Chapter X.

They are your roses, it is your garden, you and yours have to look at them — so use them as you will. A garden, it is said, should reflect something of the personality of its owners, whatever the result may be. This seems right enough, but if, like me, you cannot live with your mistakes you will not hesitate in trying to correct them. Transplantation is dealt with in Chapter XVII.

XIV

Roses as Cut Flowers

There are two and very distinct kinds of cut-flower roses. There is the bunch we cut in our garden, bury our nose in for the fragrance and then put in the house, where, to be frank, they do not last very long. Then there are the bud-like roses sold from shops and barrows that form so large a part of wedding bouquets and table decorations. Other than the fact that both types are roses there is not much connection between them.

Naturally the rose nurseryman, in the course of producing rose plants, produces flowers, but they are not sold as cut flowers, except maybe locally towards the end of the season when he is beginning to prepare the bushes for delivery. If the nurseryman is also a florist, the roses from his field will, when available, be used in the wreaths and bouquets he is asked to supply. Some may send bunches to local markets or shops, but hardly as part of an organized trade. The florists' roses are all grown under glass and are available all the year round: something is said about them later. Our prime interest is with the behaviour of roses when they are taken from the gardens to decorate our homes. As to this one must admit right away that roses, speaking generally, do not last very long, or so well as many other flowers when cut.

In *Which?* of February 1961 the Consumers' Association Ltd, in examining the efficiency of various preparations held to prolong the life of cut flowers, records that the average life of roses was 3 to 6 days compared with the 9 to 12 days of anemones, the 8 to 11 days of carnations and the 10 to 18 days of chrysanthemums. Incidentally, the Association's tests showed that no commercial preparation had any effect in prolonging the life of the cut rose. All the flowers under test were naturally shop flowers; one might reasonably expect that those cut in the garden would last longer, but the comparative result — roses a bad fourth — would no doubt be the same.

116

73. *This is how one usually sees an established bush when about to prune — rather disconcerting. Go in boldly, cut out dead and twiggy wood and prune the remaining stems to the selected degree, e.g., as here, moderately (74). Improvement on this shown in 75 — better balanced and cleaner bush.*

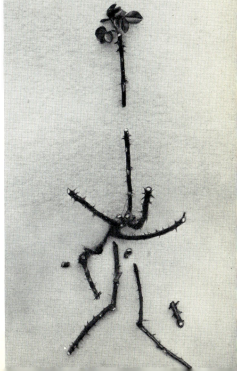

77. *Light pruning complete. The bush by the right foot and those opposite have been 'moderately' pruned.*

76. *'Light' pruning is often favoured for roses in light soil and for certain varieties, e.g., Peace. The cut is made just below the old flower stalks.*

A bowl of fresh roses will always look beautiful but the home decorator and the flower arranger (unless she is exploiting the great merits of some of the old garden roses in her art) will usually wish to use those with blooms of medium to small size commonly referred to as decorative roses carried on stiff stems, rather than the outsizes — I apologize, the not so slim.

Amateurs are usually not well equipped to conduct experiments involving comparisons — especially in the field of horticulture, where the area available to them is insufficient, time is often lacking for the constant observation required and measuring facilities and temperature control are absent. With all the reservations which this implies I give here the results of comparing the lasting powers of some of the varieties available in my garden in 1961. The hybrid teas were tested on two occasions (3 weeks apart) and as the two sets of results were so consistent, the floribundas had one test only. The varieties were those available at the time, but they were cut as near as possible at the same stage of development. They were all tested in the same room, the daily temperature of which normally ranged from 54°F to 70°F. Not more than two blooms were put in each container — a 2 lb. Kilner jar. No artificial aids to preservation were used. Stems were *not* split, hammered, immersed up to their necks for some hours after cutting or any other such capers indulged in. Thorns, however, were removed as being normal housewifely practice. Otherwise they went straight, as cut, from bush to jar. Their life was measured by reference to the day on which my wife would have thrown the bloom out had it been in the room for decorative purposes.

Here are the results, but may I emphasize again the reservation about the unscientific nature of the test.

DURATION OF CUT BLOOMS
FOUR DAYS

Hybrid Teas: Cleopatra, Spek's Yellow.

FIVE DAYS

Hybrid Teas: Beauté, Bettina, La Jolla, Lady Belper, McGredy's Yellow, Michèle Meilland, Mojave, Piccadilly, Picture, Serenade, Virgo.

Floribundas: Allgold, Dearest, Jiminy Cricket, Korona, The People, Spartan.

SIX DAYS

HYBRID TEAS: Eden Rose, Ena Harkness, Grace de Monaco, Grand Gala, Grand'mère Jenny, Helen Traubel, Konrad Adenauer, Mme Louis Laperrière, Mrs Sam McGredy, My Choice, Opera, Peace, Super Star, Sutter's Gold, The Doctor, Tzigane.

FLORIBUNDAS: Alain, Chanelle, Circus, Dainty Maid, Iceberg.

SEVEN DAYS

HYBRID TEAS: Chrysler Imperial, Golden Melody, Josephine Bruce, Karl Herbst, Margaret, Montezuma, Rose Gaujard, Silver Lining.

FLORIBUNDAS: August Seebauer, Concerto, Elsinore, Firecracker, Frensham, Lilli Marlene, Masquerade, Queen Elizabeth.

EIGHT DAYS

HYBRID TEAS: Ballet, Gail Borden, Perfecta.

FLORIBUNDAS: Rosemary Rose, Red Favourite (a double sport of this variety went to 11 days).

THE FLORISTS' ROSE

Although our particular interest is with the garden rose it may add to our enjoyment of the 'cut flower' rose to know something about it in a general kind of way. (The information given may also be of interest to the amateur who has yet to try growing roses under glass.)

The trade is highly specialized and the rose is demanding. A firm may produce other cut flowers, such as carnations and chrysanthemums, but certainly not in the same greenhouse. Roses must have their own houses, which is a tip to the amateur that he is probably not going to do very well with a pot or two of roses in a mixed greenhouse. The florist's roses are not, however, in pots but in the soil at ground level. And at that level one thing of interest is that they are not budded on to the stocks as our roses are, but are grafted. The chief disease which has to be guarded against is mildew; the red spider is the most troublesome pest.

Feeding is on much the same principles as those for outside cultivation, plenty of 'muck', that is, farmyard manure, being used. To those amateurs who favour foliar feeding it may be of interest that in the experience of at any rate one large grower this feeding by no means gives uniform results. Another illustration of the individual qualities of the rose is that under glass different varieties have different cropping seasons. This is made use of in solving the problem of meeting the public demand for an all-the-year-round supply.

I was under the impression — through not thinking about it properly — that owing to the protection of the glass and the steady and warm temperature, the greenhouse plants would give a constant supply of blooms in much greater quantity than in our gardens. It is true that on average about five crops are produced each year, but the demand for long firm stems means much disbudding so that, in the result, no more than 18 or 20 blooms per bush can be expected; there is, also, variation in the output as between one variety and another. Baccara is much in demand for its colour, a brilliant deep vermilion, but it certainly does not produce 18 blooms a year. It is also said to be a long laster.

Baccara also illustrates the point that in general the cut flower varieties are not noted for giving of their best when grown in the garden. Indeed the hybridist will try for new florists' roses. Their names are, therefore, not commonly known. There are exceptions, as usual, and among the varieties listed some have already been discussed in relation to their performance in the garden.

The scarlet crimson hybrid tea, New Yorker, has been mentioned as making a good standard: it is also a popular cut flower. Another red offered is Poinsettia, which outdoors tends to suffer from a weak neck. There is also a Red Sylvia. Among the floribundas Moulin Rouge does, as they say, a good trade.

The floribunda Garnette is a red of garnet shade and there is a bunch of hybrid teas ranging from the brilliant cerise Better Times (Aalsmeer is somewhat similar), Greta Kluis in carmine, to the deep-orange-salmon of Montezuma and the pure vermilion of Super Star. Then there are the various shades of pink — Briercliff, a deep rose, the lighter Pink Sensation and the delightful Lady Sylvia.

Good in the garden too is Nymph, a coral-salmon floribunda.

A garden hybrid tea in garish orange overlaid salmon seen in the florists will be The Queen. The floribunda Circus, yellow with pink and salmon shadings, is easy to identify.

An old standby in the yellows is the hybrid tea Geheimrat Duisberg. In much darker tone there is the aptly named Tawny Gold, of which Dr Ver Hage is a lighter edition. The creamy yellow Roselandia leads to the two whites available — Virgo and the floribunda Jewel.

There are, of course, very many millions of these florists' roses sold in this country each year — Covent Garden alone handling some 50 million blooms annually.

PART FOUR

How they are planted

The Soil and its Preparation

Feeding

Planting and Transplanting

XV

The Soil and its Preparation

WE are reaching a stage in this book when it is necessary to remind oneself of the title and of Oscar Wilde's dictum that it is better to take pleasure in a rose than put its roots under a microscope. Whether under a microscope or not the roots have certainly to be put under the soil and if one is to get the maximum enjoyment through growing good roses, it will, I think, be helpful to know something about the soil, although I am bound to say it is not a subject that I have taken to very much.

CHEMICAL CONDITION

I am with those who believe that while the texture of the soil for roses is of much importance, its chemical condition matters less. In this there is particularly in mind the business of whether the soil is alkaline or acid. This is measured by what is known as the pH scale, in this 7 is neutral, above that figure is alkaline and below is acid. Thus a reading of 3·5–4, as found in peat bogs, is very acid, while chalk being alkaline is at the other end at about 9.

It is said that roses do best in a slightly acid soil — pH 5·6–6·5. My old garden gave a reading of about 7·1, the present one is said to be 7·3. The soil at the nursery of a firm of rose nurserymen famous for the quality of their rose plants always reads over 8. I have never taken any steps to get my soil to the desirable pH of 5·6 or 6·5, although the methods of planting and, perhaps, feeding may have some effect in that direction. Obviously my soils have been tested, otherwise I could not quote figures, and if one is interested by all means have it done. There are simple testing outfits to be bought from multiple chemists, some seed merchants give a service of this kind or one's County Horticultural Officer will, without charge, arrange for a test. The last two mentioned normally include an analysis of the soil and suggest what corrective action might be desirable.

In 1959 my new garden was judged to be in the 'highest state of fertility' and a once-a-year dressing of ammonium sulphate at the rate of 2 oz. a square yard was recommended in order to encourage acidity. Did I act on the advice? Of course not. I am far too keen on growing better and, where appropriate, bigger roses to do anything so simple as that. In short I am not one whit better off from having had the soil tested. I make this confession in order to bring out that these services cost money and somebody has got to pay for them. They are of inestimable value to the farmer and nurseryman, but I suggest that the ordinary gardener does not worry about them. All I have done as a result of the expert advice is to keep lime away from the rose bed. I suggest that the ordinary rose grower does the same and forgets about pH's and all that.

Of course a statement of that kind should not be taken completely literally because if one's soil is very acid, e.g., all kinds of rhododendrons flourish, some corrective action will usually be necessary. As to this I have seen a 2 oz. to the square yard dressing of calcium carbonate (ground chalk) recommended rather than the ordinary hydrated lime.

PREPARATION OF SOIL

In making my first rose beds I faithfully followed the direction commonly given to double-dig the soil. The object of this is to break up both the top soil and the second spit, but to leave the fertile top soil at the top. Full details of double digging are in most garden books — briefly it consists, when preparing a rose bed, in removing a conveniently sized top section of soil (a spit deep), and putting it on one side. The bottom of the trench thus made, that is the second spit, is then dug and forked over and in the process there is added to it well rotted manure, leaf mould or compost, or if the bed is being dug in grass, the turf from the top. The top soil of the next section is then dug and thrown into the trench and the second spit thus revealed is treated in a similar way to that in the first section. So the process continues — the top soil from the first section which was put on one side being used to fill in the last trench. When short of the 'well rotted manure, leaf mould, etc.', I have put into or on to the second spit such things as old curtains, old clothes, newspapers, and most valuable of all (but I did not know it), the flock from an old mattress. A word must be said about the digging in of 'well rotted manure' into the second spit when dealing with heavy, usually clay, soil. Have those who tell us

More than one shoot from a
pruning cut is not a good
thing (78). If there are two, the
weaker should be removed (79).
Three shoots are common
(four less so) (80) and the two
outer ones should go. If
neglected and the shoots
develop (81), the middle one
should come out.

Neglected multiple shoots can produce a tangle (82). The result of an attempt to untangle it (83) was hardly satisfactory in itself or in relation to the bush (84) so the remaining part of the stem was cut right back to induce new growth. For this reason, and to give balance, the stem on the extreme left was also cut back.

to do it ever tried it themselves? I doubt it. How such soil might be dealt with is mentioned later.

Some people like digging, or so they say. I do not and I readily adopted an excuse to lighten the work which was given me by something I read in Mr A. Norman's *Successful Rose Growing*. As a result other beds were made by simply digging over the top spit only and incorporating into it the turf taken off the top. I was fortunate to be able to add plenty of manure or compost on both kinds of bed and they received, of course, the same artificial feeds. I never noticed any difference in the quality of roses produced.

LIGHT SOILS

Now admittedly the soil of that garden was pure sand and silt and, therefore, not a good retainer of moisture, so it was, at any rate 'in the long run' a good thing not to disturb the second spit. Had this been dug over it would have facilitated the moisture getting away. It was certainly a good thing to make the top spit more retentive by the addition of the manure and compost.

The soil of my new garden, however, is for the most part a rich greasy loam—pretty well ideal for roses—and a much larger area was planned for the rose beds. This together with lack of labour, the heavy cost of what there was available and my own antipathy to digging, precluded any double digging capers. Instead the land was ploughed at 8 in., rolled against the furrows and then worked over with a heavy rotary cultivator. Then the 'paths' were made by raking the loose soil on to the marked out beds, and thus raised them to 10 in. above the level of the 'paths' (later sown with grass seed). This level of the beds has subsequently sunk somewhat, owing to the turf gradually rotting down and reducing its volume — a point worth keeping in mind.

IMPORTANCE OF DRAINAGE

A large operation of this kind does not, I am well aware, interest the owner of an average-sized garden. But I have brought it in to help illustrate two important points, which hold good whether one has 8 or 800 square yards of rose beds. The first is one held to by all the experts: roses must have good drainage. If there is none or little they will drown, because the water will remain in the soil and so fill up all the air spaces in it. On the other hand if there is too much drainage as, for example, in the very sandy soils, there will be an absence of moisture. And as plants can only assimilate nourishment when it is dissolved in water, its absence means that they will starve.

What one needs, therefore, is a proper balance in the soil between aeration and moisture retention. It seems to me that, in digging over the second spit of the beds in my first garden, I was going out of my way to increase the porosity of soil already too porous, and reversing the process by adding the manure, flock, and so on. The process with the much heavier soil in the new garden was more rational in that the level of the beds was raised (with top, that is, fertile soil) well above the surrounding levels and in this way I made sure that the roses were clear of the non-porous clay which lay beneath the first spit at the existing level.

IMPORTANCE OF THE TOP SPIT

This leads on to the second point, namely, that given proper drainage, it is what happens in and to the top 8 or 10 in. of the rose bed which really matters. In my experience the modern rose, reasonably well fed and drained, does not send down long tap roots. Indeed in planting we are enjoined to cut back such roots to encourage the production of fibrous roots because it is roots of this kind that do the feeding; the more that top spit is aerated and spongelike so as to carry moisture, and hence food, the better. Before enlarging on this there is something that must be said about soil preparation in relation to heavy clays and to chalk.

HEAVY CLAY

I have been fortunate in my two rose gardens but I have a lively recollection of the hard labour involved in making a garden, including rose beds, in the heavy clay of North-West London. I should then have welcomed my present knowledge that the second spit in such soil must positively be broken up and kept opened up. The trouble about clay soil is that owing to the fineness of its constituent particles there is little air between them and, hence, little room for moisture either to get in or to get out. The absence of air means lack of oxygen, without which the organic material in the soil cannot decompose and provide plant food, while as already explained the absence of moisture prevents the plant from absorbing what food there is.

Accordingly it is necessary to change the structure of clay soil so that the minute particles stick together so as to form larger and permanent crumbs of soil. In the latter connection it may have been noticed that those crumbs into which well dug clay falls, after exposure to frosts and winds, soon break down again after heavy rains into the typical solid mass.

The sticking together of the fine particles is called flocculation. Hydrated lime is the agent usually recommended to bring it about and it has to be forked into the second spit as far as it is possible to do so, and not just sprinkled on the surface. The rate recommended is 3 lb. to the square yard. Some experts on the subject hold that lime is slow in its flocculating action and its effect is of limited duration. Instead they suggest the use of gypsum (calcium sulphate; lime is calcium hydroxide) as being both quicker and more permanent. About 1 lb. to the square yard, raked into the forked top 2 in. or so, is recommended. This sounds far more practical than trying to fork it in deeply. Gypsum likes rain to get it into action, so presumably one should not be in a hurry to put the top spit back.

CHALK SOILS

As I have no experience of chalk soil I here rely entirely on the wisdom of others. Some of them hold that there are enough plants and flowers taking to chalk naturally to make the use of roses unnecessary.

But Sir Frederick Stern in his chalkpit garden at Highdown, Sussex, grows successfully, in addition to many species roses, such varieties as Goldilocks, Alain, Masquerade, Mermaid and New Dawn without excessive measures against the chalk.

Gardens on chalk usually have only a few inches of real soil on the top of the solid chalk, which provides too much drainage. This is an almost hopeless proposition: those who want roses, especially hybrid teas, must face up to the challenge of providing at least 12 in. of soil, and this may involve importation. But as long as humus is added heavily and steadily chalk gardeners find that most of the rose varieties commonly grown can still be relied on — if properly fed and frequently watered. The most common trouble on chalk is chlorosis, shown by yellowing of the leaves (see page 166).

HUMUS OF PRIME IMPORTANCE

We come now to the all-important subject of humus — 'the amorphous black substance which results from the decay of vegetable matter in soil at a certain stage' — and without which that top soil is not going to give of its best in the way of roses or, for that matter, any other plants. The functions of humus are, it seems, varied and technical, but for ordinary gardeners like ourselves, it is sufficient for us to know that, by helping to build up the bacterial population, it improves the physical condition of the soil by making it retentive of moisture and receptive of plant foods. In addition to providing some food in itself, that is, by returning to the soil what has come out, it produces the conditions necessary for the assimilation of other foods — whether organic or chemical. In short humus puts the soil into 'good heart'.

In most cultivated gardens humus will already be present in the soil, having come from decayed weeds, flowers and leaves. In new gardens, which often means those where the builder has left rubble and has removed the top spit of soil, it will have to be introduced. In both types and in those which vary in between these two extremes, the humus content will have to be maintained.

COMPOST HEAP

A prime source of ready made humus is, of course, the matured compost heap. The important word is 'matured', for only in such a heap will be seen the 'amorphous black substance'. It is not part of the business of this book to explain how to make compost. If you do not know ask any gardening friend who has a compost heap, how he does it. He will be delighted to tell you. But do not ask more than one, because composting is a highly individual art, and each compostor seems to be his own fanatic on the subject. Alternatively, consult any practical gardening book.

Among other bulky organic materials from which satisfactory humus can be produced are farmyard manure, leaf mould, spent hops, peat and shoddy. Normally all of them, including compost, are best put on the rose beds as a mulch, that is, a thin covering about 2 in. thick — naturally farmyard manure will be thicker. April or May is the best time. In the following autumn (or even as late as just before the next dressing is given in the following year), it should be lightly forked into the soil.

FARMYARD MANURE

Farmyard manure as a source of humus material is mentioned first because for the large majority of gardeners it is unobtainable — so it seems better to get it out of the way. What may be useful to say is that its humus value comes from the straw element, although this is enhanced by the animal solids and moisture. If it is any comfort to those who cannot get a supply, I say that it does not enhance the look of the rose beds and it is a constant and indefatigable provider of untidiness owing to the birds picking at the straw and depositing it on the paths — grass or otherwise — between the beds. However, if one can get it be sure it is at least one year old and weed-free.

LEAF MOULD

Leaf mould I have found to be satisfactory provided it is quite rotted down, that is, all the leaves have completely disintegrated. Mats of half rotted leaves stuck together prevent the air getting to the soil and they can also be a source of untidiness, especially when winds are high. Moreover, the potential food value of leaf mould is said to be low. On the whole, for our purposes, dead leaves are best used as part of the material for the compost heap.

SPENT HOPS AND SHODDY

Spent hops and shoddy — the latter made from scrap wool in various forms (it is assumed that the source of spent hops is common knowledge) — are both rather 'local' products, but I have seen shoddy advertised in the gardening press. Spent hops are not the same thing as 'hop manure', which is produced by the addition of fertilizers to the hops. I have no personal experience of either shoddy or spent hops, but a successful rose growing friend has used spent hops and found them very satisfactory. I would not know whether there is any connection between this success and the practice of a local innkeeper who enlivens two slothful climbers by giving them the lees from the beer barrels.

PEAT

Much can be written about peat and its importance in horticulture. It is the answer for the manureless and compostless gardener, whether he has just a few well cared for roses or is growing in a larger way. It is equally important, if not more so, as a planting material (see Chapter XVII). Like spent hops and the rest, peat is not humus in itself: it has to acquire that status through decay. In the meantime, however, it acts as an excellent soil conditioner since, coming as it does from plant remains, it is practically entirely organic matter. It is especially noted for its water capacity which can be up to twelve times its own weight or up to 95 per cent of its own bulk.

There are two main types — sedge peat, formed from reeds and

I

sedges, is a very dark brown, and almost black when moist; and moss peat, which, as its name suggests, comes from mosses. Both types have acid reactions; that of the sedge peat is said to be a good deal less than that of the moss kind. They each have a certain amount of mineral matter — the moss less than the sedge—but this supply of plant 'food' is relatively unimportant: the value of peat lies in the physical properties.

Each kind has its uses. I have used both from various sources and for roses I prefer sphagnum moss peat — large supplies of which are in Ireland — as it does not readily powder when handled and can dry out without diminishing its capacity to take up moisture again. In particular the sponge-like quality seems more developed in the sphagnum moss than in the sedge. Moreover it appears to disintegrate more slowly in the soil, thus preserving the good aeration and moisture retention for a longer period. Other advantages of peat as a humus-making material is its initial freedom from weed seeds and from pests and diseases. As a mulch it is an effective damper of all but the most vigorous weeds, such as convolvulus, and it gives rather a pleasant appearance to the rose beds.

All good things have to be paid for: compared with the compost heap or such things as spent hops peat is not all that cheap. Owing to the moisture factor it is best bought by volume rather than by weight. To put a covering of say 2 in. on a rose bed of say 24 ft. by 6 ft. will need 8 bushels of the moss type (cost is given in Chapter XXI).

GREEN MANURING

There is another form of soil conditioning — or rather reconditioning which must be mentioned, namely green manuring. It is of importance in relation to roses and really amounts to compost making in the beds themselves. One often hears the complaint that when a new rose bush is put into an old established bed to take the place of one that has died, it fails to do well. The reason is that the soil is rose sick, just as soil can be pansy sick or petunia sick. Before a replacement is put in about a cubic foot of soil should be removed and replaced from some other part of the garden. But at some time or another the whole bed may need to be replaced on account of rose sickness. In very old gardens such as one gets in the centre of London and other cities the soil — invariably dark and dusty — is sick of everything and needs renewing or rejuvenating.

The answer is green manuring. It must be faced, however, that this means no roses for a year because their place will be taken by one, two or even three crops of mustard, vetches, or tares. The first crop will be sown (once ounce or more to the square yard) in the spring. Agricultural mustard is the kind required and it will grow rather larger than those seedlings we use in sandwiches and such like. When the main stems are finger thick the crop should be flattened down and dug right into the top soil. Another sowing should follow at once. Some people use an accelerator on the flattened plants before digging in, but I have not found it necessary myself. A good watering before turning in will, however, keep up the process of decay. The second (or third crop) should have been dug in by mid-November and roses may be planted again in the following February or March — preceded by the addition to the soil of 4 oz. of fish manure or bone meal to the square yard. Mr Bertram Park, an outstanding authority, favours seeding at the rate of 5 oz. of cocksfoot grass and ½ oz. of red clover to each square yard instead of the mustard, etc. I have mentioned: this is on the ground that the roots of the cocksfoot are depth seekers and will thus break up and aerate the soil. Another authority recommends Italian rye grass, sown at ½ oz. per square yard, as a particularly good plant for the purpose because of the extensive fibrous root system it makes, which improves soil texture remarkably well.

XVI

Feeding

'ROSES are gross feeders': how often one sees this statement. And do we really understand what it means? A 'gross feeder' is one who likes coarse, greasy, unclean and repulsive food! I suppose that what is meant is that roses require a lot of food.

On the other side there are those who seem to think that roses need no nourishment at all. I am surprised by the number of people who, though they take a real interest in their gardens, say — 'But you feed your roses' as though one was not playing fair.

The truth lies between these extremes. Roses, like most other things in the garden, respond to feeding.

In the previous chapter it was said that humus was essential to the soil and that humus makers were organic material such as peat, spent hops and the compost heap. The humus makers do not, however, contain a great deal of plant food: what there is is rather slow acting and not particularly well balanced. They need, therefore, to be supplemented if our garden plants, including, of course, the roses, are to give of their best: this is where plant food in the form of fertilizers comes in. The humus makers and the fertilizers are complementary to each other.

ESSENTIAL PLANT FOODS

The essential plant foods are many — about a dozen, ranging from nitrogen to boron. Most of them are needed in very small quantities only and are, therefore, called 'trace elements'. These will be present already in most soils or will get there through adding humus or balanced fertilizers; there is, therefore, no need to enumerate them here in detail or to worry too much about them in relation to our roses. Nitrogen, however, is another matter as this, together with phosphates and potash, forms a triple alliance of really important and essential plant foods. They are commonly written as N for nitrogen, P for phosphate, and K for potash.

85. *Hybrid teas moderately pruned early in January 1961, were as shown at the end of March — a long accepted date for pruning in the south. 86. Another batch of the same variety, unpruned until that time, is clearly carrying much more foliage, all of which was wasted — 87 when the moderate pruning was done.*

88. *Aphides (greenfly) in operation and the results therefrom — bud (left) practically destroyed and stem of bloom (right) bent unnaturally.* 89. *Very hard pruning, i.e., to 1 in. — an American suggestion for preventing the 'carry-over' of black spot disease to the next season.*

90. *A sequel to a very severe attack of black spot can be the dying back of much (and sometimes the whole) of the plant in the next spring or early summer.*

In relation to our roses the phosphates will help ensure the production of roots — themselves essential in order to enable the plant to take in food — and it will also hasten the production of blooms. Potash goes to make the blooms, enhances their colour and helps the plant to resist diseases. Nitrogen is the leaf maker, without which the rose plant will not get very far because the foliage is the means through which it breathes and absorbs the sun's rays. The latter are essential to enable the plant to transform and absorb the foods. And no matter how well the soil is stocked with foods before we put in our roses, they will need to be replaced. How is this to be done?

ORGANIC AND INORGANIC FERTILIZERS

We can use organic, or what might be termed natural fertilizers such as farmyard manure, compost, bone meal, dried blood, hoof and horn or fish meal. Or we can feed inorganically by using chemical salts, usually termed artificial fertilizers, such as sulphate of ammonia, superphosphate of lime and sulphate of potash.

There was a time, and it may still be present, when arguments about the relative merits of organics (the compostors leading) and inorganics for fertilizing one's garden were so fierce that neighbours ceased to be neighbourly and season ticket holders changed from their customary railway carriage. Truth, as so often, lies with both sides. Both types have their uses. Save for dried blood, the organics are slow in acting: the inorganics are quick. There is also general agreement that as a basis well rotted farmyard manure and garden compost are excellent, especially when dug in before planting or when used as a mulch and dug in later. But so few of us can come by the farmyard manure and some of us lack time or facilities for making compost. We must therefore rely on other fertilizers.

It may, therefore, be useful to say something of what the various organics and inorganics supply in the way of the three essential foods and the more important trace elements.

ORGANICS

Bone meal gives — phosphate
Meat and bone meal gives — nitrogen with phosphate and iron
Fish meal gives — phosphate, nitrogen, potash, boron
Hoof and horn gives — nitrogen
Dried blood gives — nitrogen
Wood ash (fresh) gives — potash

INORGANICS

The inorganics suffer from some elegant variation in their names. It is the uninitiated gardener who suffers through wondering whether a variation refers to a different chemical, so in the following list the variations are bracketed together:

Superphosphate
Superphosphate of calcium
Calcium superphosphate } gives phosphate
Superphosphate of lime

Ammonium sulphate
Sulphate of ammonia } gives nitrogen

Potassium nitrate
Nitrate of potash } gives nitrogen and potash
Nitrate of potassium

Potassium sulphate
Sulphate of potash } gives potash
Sulphate of potassium

Magnesium sulphate
Sulphate of magnesia } gives magnesium
Epsom salts

Iron sulphate
Sulphate of iron } gives iron

Calcium sulphate
Sulphate of calcium } gives calcium
Gypsum

FERTILIZERS FOR ROSES

Over the years I have made a collection of the feeding formulas of many experienced rose growers. Most of them use each year a first dressing of bone meal or meat and bone meal in February or early March, but thereafter there is great diversity in the diets offered.

Here are some examples, the information given earlier may help people to evaluate them. The numbers represent the parts by weight in each mixture and practically all of them are distributed at the rate of 4 oz. to the square yard.

A Superphosphate (P) 7
  Dried blood (N) 7
  Potassium sulphate (K) 4
  Bone meal (P) 7

B Superphosphate (P) 8
  Ammonium sulphate (N) 16
  Potassium sulphate (K) 8
  Iron sulphate 4
  Magnesium sulphate 4

C Superphosphate (P) 8
  Potassium sulphate (K) 3
  Ammonium sulphate (N) 2

D Superphosphate (P) 2
  Ammonium sulphate (N) 1
  Potassium sulphate (K) 1
  (plus fish manure late July)

E Superphosphate (P) 2
  Meat and bone meal
            (N & P) 4
  Potassium sulphate (K) 1

F Superphosphate (P) 7
  Ammonium sulphate (N) $2\frac{1}{2}$
  Potassium sulphate (K) 5
  Magnesium sulphate 5

G Superphosphate (P) 16
  Potassium nitrate
            (N & K) 6
  Ammonium sulphate (N) 3
  Potassium sulphate (K) 8
  Magnesium sulphate 2
  Iron sulphate $\frac{1}{2}$

H Superphosphate (P) 12
  Potassium nitrate
            (N & K) 10
  Magnesium sulphate 2
  Iron sulphate 1
  Calcium sulphate 8

J A handful of superphosphate and spent hops. (Short and sweet or, perhaps, short and bitter?)

One's first reaction is 'They cannot all be right'. But if they grow good roses for the user they must be so. Some may well be due to personal preferences, but most will have been found by experience to suit best the soil and growing conditions of the user's garden — mixture 'C' for instance is used on loam with a clay sub-soil.

If the parts by weight were put onto a common multiple, I think it would be found that the proportions of N, P and K are as diverse as the ingredients. This may reflect the diversity of the soils, but more likely it shows the diversity of opinion as to what these proportions should be in a quick acting fertilizer for roses. What are we ordinary people to do? G is the mixture currently recommended by the National Rose Society for application following the 4 oz. to the square yard of meat and bone meal which is put on in early spring. In it the N P K proportions are broadly 1 : 2 : 1.

For my part I have used this mixture with satisfaction for many years. One has, of course, to make it for oneself. But lately I have felt an urge to use more of the organics and less of the inorganics. In this nearly a full circle has been turned because in my early days I used fish manure entirely. The urge is not based on any scientific reason, although the organics tend to improve the general condition of the soil and are less liable to be leached out by rain. It is rather on the basis that with my high-fertility soil the slow-acting fertilizers are the more useful as they provide a steady replacement and they are, so far as I can see, the most economical in cost. In cost I include convenience of handling and storage in that, for example, although the N P K of fish manure is 1 :1 :1 and perhaps not just right by some standards for roses, it is however very suitable for general garden use. It may be of interest that I made my return to fish manure before realising that fish meal, its basic element, contained so many of the essential plant foods. Fish manure includes a small portion of inorganics in order to obtain a complete balance. This, I understand, is also true of other organic mixtures. On the rose beds fish manure has no objectionable smell, but in the store shed, unless well covered, I fear that it will be found that the fish has lost its savour. One cannot have everything.

The use of fish manure as the basic feed does not mean that no quick acting inorganics are used. Mixture 'H' is the make-up of a celebrated and long standing fertilizer for roses — Tonk's Rose Manure. It contains practically all the essential minerals mentioned earlier and is for all practical purposes a completely balanced mixture. I have been using it for the past two years when I think it necessary, for example, as a special tonic following a bad attack of black spot and as a boost for the second flush of bloom from such varieties as Lady Belper and La Jolla, which are inclined to come on the small side. Tonk's undoubtedly gives its best results on moderately heavy loam, such as that in my garden. Tonk's can be purchased ready made but I do not think it is widely available, so that one may have to make it up oneself.

Long before now you will have been saying that all these various kinds of food and mixtures are all very well for those with large numbers of roses and for those who like to make up their own fertilizers: what about those who cannot be bothered or whose requirements are small? Many rose nurserymen make up their own balanced mixtures and offer them to their customers. These can, of course, be relied upon provided they are used as directed. There are, too, a number of proprietary rose fertilizers readily available of which, in addition to fish manure, at least two are mainly organic. All can be purchased in convenient packs and those I have tried have given good results.

Having selected a mixture or a particular brand of fertilizer it is, I suggest, only common sense and fair to give the selection a trial for two or three seasons and not to judge on one year only, especially in view of the variations in our summers and in local conditions. Do not, however, be afraid to experiment within reason. It is *not* within reason, however, to vary the maker's directions when using a proprietary fertilizer.

If you decide to use an inorganic mixture such as that recommended by the National Rose Society ('G', page 135), you will probably wish to follow its recommendation that meat and bone meal should be scattered on the beds at the rate of two good handfuls to the square yard in the early spring. My own view, which I believe is shared by some others, is that owing to its slow action the meat and bone meal (or, if unobtainable, bone meal) should go on a good deal earlier. In this connection one must remember the wide range of dates when the true growing spring begins (page 93). There are advocates for putting on the meal in November as part of the autumn cleaning-up operations. As an early pruner I used to put it on each bed as the pruning was completed. Normally this meant that it was all on by about mid-January. A good working rule is, probably, the heavier the soil the earlier the application.

A word about 'meat and bone meal' and 'bone meal' may be helpful. On page 133 it shows that the latter produces phosphates, but the former gives nitrogen and iron in addition. Hence the preference. But unfortunately while bone meal is, in my experience, readily obtainable, meat and bone meal is less so and usually has to be ordered specially. This is a further consideration which has inclined me towards the balanced organic fertilizers such as fish manure because they give all that the bone meal has and much more too.

My fish manure practice is, therefore, to put on 4 to 6 oz. per square yard immediately after pruning, followed by a further 2 oz. when the first buds appear. I think it will be found that the recommended use of the proprietary rose fertilizers based on organics follows much the same idea — such as 4 oz. early in the spring followed by half that quantity each month during the following period.

Reference has been made to scattering the fertilizers on the beds. Naturally they vary in weight somewhat, but a rough guide is that a single handful is about 2 oz. 'Scattering' is the operative word, because the roots are not just immediately around the stem. Foliage can be harmed if the inorganic fertilizers come into contact with it, and if this happens a shake of the bush will usually get most of it off. It is useful to 'prick in' the fertilizer with a fork or to hoe it in lightly. This means precisely what it says: the hair roots come quite near the surface and they may easily be damaged if the fork or hoe goes more than 1 or 2 in. down.

FOLIAR FEEDING

No explanation about feeding roses can be complete without a reference to foliar feeding. The exploitation of the capacity of a plant's foliage to take in food in liquid form was first practised by Mr F. A. Secret in 1922, in this country. The idea was exported to U.S.A. and has now returned here as a new idea (not the first time that something like this has happened).

Mr Seymour Heatley achieved some remarkable results from foliar feeding in his Dublin garden where the soil was very old and deficient and which had not responded to normal methods for its improvement. His roses took premier awards in London and elsewhere until, unfortunately, ill-health prevented him from exhibiting. For a number of years, using the same American proprietary preparation as Mr Heatley, I have supplemented my normal feeding in this way. I have also experimented with the same chemicals as he used when making up his own mixture. Proprietary foliar feeds are now marketed in this country and I have been using one of them. I have also used the 'do it yourself' formula suggested by the National Rose Society, which is two parts by weight of urea and one part of potassium acid phosphate at the combined rate of ½ oz. to a gallon of water. These ingredients can be obtained from most large chemists. The use of a 'wetting' or spreading agent in the solution to break down the surface tension of the leaves is essential when using foliar feeds and both sides of the leaves should be sprayed.

It may encourage people to experiment with foliar feeds to know that they can normally be used as part of the spraying operations against pests and diseases. And it is this 'ease of application' which makes me continue to foliar-feed. I have no proof, however, that the growth of my roses is any more due to foliar feeding than to the soil and to the foods given in the normal way. I have no doubt whatever of its success in Mr Heatley's garden and I have myself seen weakly bushes brought to health by it. My conclusion, so far, is that in certain conditions it can be an excellent supplementary feed, especially in the production of good foliage.

A further thought on feeding one's roses is that fertilizers will not make up for cultural faults, such as indifferent preparation of the soil, bad planting and inattention to preventive spraying. Nor can they counteract the effect of bad weather — although I have read that an application of 2 oz. per square yard of potassium sulphate will help to make up for a lack of sun. Properly used, however, they will help to keep the soil in condition, to produce healthier plants and better roses.

And finally, gross feeders or not, roses can only use a certain amount of food; excessive applications of fertilizers will not give still bigger and better blooms. On the contrary it means waste of money and it may do positive harm by 'locking up' the essential trace elements — that is, preventing the roses from making use of them.

XVII

Planting and Transplanting

WE all like parcels: most of us get a kick when opening one even though we may be well aware of what will be inside. But of all parcels, those straw-covered bundles containing trees, shrubs and roses seem, at any rate to the gardener, to give the most pleasure. This may be owing to the straw, redolent of the countryside and its golden-yellow fields, or to the consciousness that the contents of the bundle have so much beauty and pleasure stored away for the future. What a quantity of useful twine or cord is used and what a quantity of knots, which seem to be specially devised to baffle and to discourage their undoing, so that, patience exhausted, knife or secateurs rip along and one can plunge through the straw. The number of standards I have damaged by hauling them out by the root end instead of first carefully removing the straw round the heads is nobody's business.

NEW METHODS OF PACKING

And that straw: how moist it keeps the contents; what a useful addition to the compost heap; how splendid a lighter for the autumn bonfire. Alas! Make the most of it, for in the rose world it is fast disappearing in favour of nothing more romantic than polythene, paper bags or boxes — so economical of labour for the rose nursery-man, so mundane for the recipient, but I fear just as an effective form of delivery as that straw. In the spring of 1961, I deliberately left such a parcel containing half-a-dozen roses unopened for exactly one month in a half-open porch exposed to the northerly winds. When opened the roses were alive and kicking. They had produced a few very pale shoots; not a very desirable feature as they would have to be pruned off, so that they were to some extent wasting the plants' energy, but really nothing to worry about. More important, however, the highly desirable hair roots were getting well away. But I still hanker after that straw, despite the fact that the gardener, a retired

91. The most effective form of spraying is a fine mist such as shown here, not only on top but also — 92. right into the centre of the bushes, especially where black spot is concerned, because it is the mature leaves low down in the plant which are most open to attack.

93. *Mulching is an excellent thing to conserve moisture, and later, when lightly forked in, to improve the soil's texture. Compost when fully mature is excellent material, but not if, as here, it is immature — especially in a wet summer.*

cowman and very 'foot and mouth' conscious, insists on its being burnt.

TREATMENT ON ARRIVAL — 'HEELING IN'

Many rose nurserymen, in their catalogues, or when acknowledging or sending one's order, give hints about how to treat the roses on arrival. One cannot do better than follow this advice. Clearly the sooner the package is open and the new arrivals are in the ground, the better. Frost, snow, sodden ground or lack of immediately available time may clearly say wait. So if impatience to see the plants can be curbed, leave the package unopened. Sheltered from frost and, if in straw, moistened by a bucket of water, they will be quite safe for up to a fortnight. If, however, adverse conditions are likely to be prolonged, then open up and 'heel' the plants in by making a shallow trench, laying the roots therein and covering them and the lower part of the stems with soil, which should be lightly firmed down. But before so doing remember that water and worms play havoc with paste-board labels which are invariably tied on at the base of the plant, and replace them with something more permanent. Do not imagine that the paste-board labels will last the few days or weeks you estimate the heeling-in will last. They will not, because your estimate will most probably be wrong. You may have to drive yourself to do this tedious job on a wet or cold Saturday, but make the effort as I did not, even after twelve years, with a parcel of shrub and old roses, and so had to spend precious hours in the summer trying to identify them from the catalogue. In this connection nurserymen seem to be modernizing their labels too by replacing their thin paste-board with plastic material.

Heeled in, effectively labelled or otherwise, the bushes will remain in excellent condition for a long time especially if one has removed any foliage still on the plants. I had some 600 kept thus for over four months in the winter of 1958–1959. Should, however, something go wrong as it once did with me when I opened a parcel to get out a particular variety and then left the remainder completely exposed for three months, do not despair if your plants have dried out and shrivelled up, Plate 44. Bury them *completely* about a spit deep, Plate 45, and they will be completely restored, Plate 47. If there is failure to mark the burial spot (Plate 46), much time may be wasted in locating the body, as I know from bitter experience.

IMPORTANCE OF PLANTING OPERATION

It may be felt that in light of the obvious toughness of rose plants much of what has been written so far is so much 'fuss-pottery', but I am afraid this theme will continue because I regard proper planting as a much more important element in successful rose growing than many other things which we are enjoined to do: in my view proper planting is more important than forking over that second spit of soil when preparing the beds. Moreover, it is surely worth while taking trouble over a plant which, normally, will be good for at least twelve years?

In 1959 I planted out some twelve hundred roses of various kinds: the operation began on March 28 (Boat Race Day) and did not finish until near the end of May. The dry summer of 1959 is not likely to be forgotten. Not ten plants were lost. This result is attributed to good preparation of the top spit of soil and, more particularly, to the use of a mixture of moist peat moss and meat and bone meal as the main planting medium. It must not be inferred from this that I am suggesting that the rose planting season runs from end of October to the end of May. The earlier they are in the better, but so long as the soil and the weather permit, one is certainly safe enough up to the first week in April (Plate 36). I have a lively and most pleasurable memory of planting beds of Lady Sylvia and Crimson Glory in mid-March 1952 and having them in full bloom on May 25. Admittedly that spring was exceptional, but what season of the year is unexceptional in this country? I have, however, one reservation as to spring planting: it is that some varieties of standards put in late in the season do not seem to 'get away' like the rose bushes do and in consequence growth and flowers can be very disappointing. To a lesser degree this can also be said about some of the climbers, especially the sports of the hybrid teas.

PLANTING MIXTURE

The planting mixture I have mentioned is the one recommended by the National Rose Society. A double handful of meat and bone meal is added to a three-gallon bucket of moist peat and mixed in. By the way, most domestic galvanized buckets are just three gallons, and the smaller plastic ones are one gallon. The mixing is best done in the wheelbarrow or some other larger receptacle; also the more readily obtainable bone meal can be used instead of the meat and bone meal. In this connection it will, I think, be found that makers of proprietary brands of organic manures suggest that 4 to 6 oz. per square yard be dug in to the top spit before the planting of a bed begins. If this is done then the meat and bone meal can be omitted from the mixture. Above all *do not* use the inorganic fertilizers in the mixture as they can affect the young roots adversely — this goes too for the balanced organic mixtures, which as already indicated usually contain some inorganics.

Before planting begins the plants will need a little attention. If the foliage is still on — early arrivals will often have flower buds too — it should be removed. Unripened stems, being the late growth, should be removed (they look lighter in colour and feel 'lightweight') and any longish roots should be reduced to 8 or 10 in. so as to encourage fibrous growth. Also look to see whether the nurseryman has removed the stump of the root stock just above the union (see Plate 14) and if he has not cut if off with the secateurs as near to the main stem as possible.

The roots of standards on rugosa stock may need a little special attention. The roots of this stock like to be near the surface of the soil, but it may be found that the root system consists of several tiers, taking six or more inches of the stem. The upper tiers, that is, those above about 2 in. from the bottom, should be removed. This characteristic of the rugosa stock also means that the standard should not be deeply planted, which is all the more reason for getting in its stake before that operation begins. (I prefer any form of old iron as a stake to one of wood and I use ordinary black insulating tape — eight or nine turns — instead of sacking and cord.)

Pruning before planting only arises as regards bushes and standards if planting takes place in the spring and it is dealt with in the next Chapter.

Finally, if happily the planting operation is to be 'straight from package to bed', it will be very beneficial to immerse the roots in water for an hour or so. It follows that during the actual planting work the roots of the plants waiting attention should be kept covered with a sack or something to prevent them drying out. This is most important and, of course, applies also to plants which have been heeled in.

THE PLANTING OPERATION

Provided with plants, sack, spade or flat tined fork (a very useful implement) and planting mixture, we are ready to begin: but first it may be useful to peg out the positions in the bed that the bushes are going to occupy.

There are schools which favour making a hole with a raised mound in the centre and those which prefer a sloping hole. Without subscribing to the all-too-easy 'dig a hole and shove it in' attitude I rather think that the kind of nicety I have mentioned tends to be over-done. A hole of rather over a foot in diameter seems about right, with sufficient depth to ensure that the union — the fattish knobbly junction between the root stock and the rose proper (see Plate 64) — will be at the level of the bed when the job is complete. After very little experi-ence one can judge this depth almost exactly. One will still get some lovely blooms if it is not exact, but do not be so slap-dash as to get the result shown in Plate 49. Both the bushes shown were put in at the same time (in April 1959): the one on the left very badly indeed as the union is nearly 2 in. above ground level: the other plant was put in correctly. Compare the results two years later.

To return to our hole: put into it a couple of handfuls of the plant-ing mixture and finger into it some of the loose soil. Insert the bush and spread out the roots evenly if you can, but do not worry if, be-cause they are all pointing one way as in Plate 64, this cannot be done completely. Just do what can be done — it is quite unnecessary to shout for one's wife to help because you want two hands to keep the roots spread out. I have never noticed that the quality of the plant and its blooms suffer because the roots were not fanned out like the frame of an umbrella.

Having put the plant in the hole go on adding the mixture and soil in alternate handfuls, giving the plant an occasional shake to let the soil and mixture get among the roots. When the hole is becoming full start to firm lightly with hands or foot, adding mixture and soil as necessary, and finish by treading firmly, working from the outside of the hole towards the centre — the reverse process will lower the plant. (This is sometimes a useful get-out if the hole has not been made quite deep enough!) Fork over lightly and if all is well the top of the union will be level with the soil.

This description assumes that the soil is in just the right condition: it will probably not be so. Planting in very heavy soil will be more satisfactory if more peat is used in addition to that of the mixture. If the soil is very wet and sticky and planting cannot wait, then the 'tread in' should be done very lightly indeed and one should wait until the drying winds have put things right before finally firming in.

95. *The vigorous and ever changing Masquerade in its second season is a good example of floribundas as standards.*

94. *Allgold and a hybrid tea type floribunda, The People, which here is fully open. A good pair cheek to cheek.*

96. *Kordesii and other climbers, shrubs and tall growing roses — Leverküsen, Zwei-brücken, Elmshorn, Berlin, Queen Elizabeth, Buccaneer and Danse du Feu.*
97. *Blooms from the shrub border (left to right) — Maigold (climber); Frühlingsmorgen (find the bee), Frühlingsgold (very light yellow) and Canary Bird.*

In connection with both these points some people take steps to keep a supply of dry soil under shelter, which they add to the mixture — half and half.

Really the job of planting is quite straightforward — Plates 50 to 57 show it from A to Z — and it is certainly worth a little special trouble. It will be noticed that the bush in the plates is already pruned: this is because the planting operation was done in the spring (see page 151).

TRANSFERRING ROSES

The planning and arranging of the rose garden and the contents of the rose beds offer many opportunities for mistakes and one should not be afraid to correct them. Indeed it is not only a question of real errors but also of changing ideas and tastes as one's garden develops. And is change for change's sake so very dreadful? There is very little in the ordinary run of gardening, when it comes to the point, which cannot be moved satisfactorily. Certainly roses of all kinds can be transplanted with ease and little likelihood of loss. Indeed some people hold that they respond to a little root pruning just as fruit trees do and the removal of an established plant will almost inevitably mean that its long tap roots, if any, will be severed. Naturally, the longer the rose has been growing the greater the likelihood of a large and strong root system. It is better therefore to recognize one's mistakes as soon as possible.

The recommended time for transfers is the end of October, but I have never felt particularly bound by that date. With practice and knowledge of the soil in the garden one gets to know pretty well when the moisture conditions will ensure that a good ball of soil will adhere to the roots. The important thing to aim for is a minimum disturbance of the fibrous root system and a great help in achieving this is not to be frightened of the operation and, therefore, fidgety.

Dig a hole about a foot square and a spade's depth at the new site. Then boldly make four spade cuts, at a slight incline and to the full depth of the spade, round the bush and about a foot from it. These cuts will usually have cut through the longer roots. Instead of taking the spade out after the fourth cut use it to lever out and carry the plant to the new bed. Then, slide it gently into the hole, using the spade to ease it into a completely upright position. If you like put in some of the standard planting mixture to fill up any spaces, but it is not essential. Finally firm in carefully so that the bush remains at its old level, and get on with the next one. If, however, the ball of soil or

K

most of it drops off, as it sometimes will, just as you are congratulating yourself on success, do not worry: just continue by planting out in the ordinary way with the planting mixture. At worst the plant in question will take a little longer to re-establish itself. Plates 58 to 63 show the operation.

What has been said applies equally to standards and climbers: a little assistance may be necessary with them and well developed climbers should be wrapped round with twine or rope to get them under control. Several climbers of eight years old were thus moved from my old garden and they did not — I admit, much to my surprise — die back an inch.

Probably you will develop your own transfer technique, but there is one thing which must be done, no matter at what time of the year you make the transfer or what kind of rose is involved in it: *all the foliage must be removed.* And how you will hate it if you leave the transfer to the spring when all the glorious new foliage will have to come off. Grim and recent experience makes me enjoin this upon you most earnestly. If that foliage is not removed it continues to transpire — to 'breathe out' water vapour — and thus sucks moisture from stems and roots. Since the roots are incapable of taking in water till they have grown new root hairs, the plant rapidly dies of desiccation. An added precaution in a spring operation — if there is a dry spell — is to water the plants thoroughly — at least a gallon for bushes, two for standards and shrub roses and three for climbers.

May our planting mistakes grow less but our skill at transplanting increase.

PART FIVE

How they are looked after

Pruning

Pests and Diseases

Spraying, Cultivation and Maintenance

XVIII

Pruning

SOME years back I ventured to give a talk on roses in the village hall. Conscientious to a degree I dug up and took with me a standard rose and towards the end of the allotted time I gave a practical demonstration of pruning. It must have been done with some aplomb, though certainly not with skill, as it earned a spontaneous and loud round of applause which quite staggered and elated me. The time for questions followed immediately thereafter, whereupon a wretched schoolboy — I regret to say it was my son — got up and asked 'Why are roses pruned?' Did I know or could I remember the answer? Of course not. The lifemanship reply given was 'A very good question. I well remember that the year I forgot to prune my mother's roses they produced the finest display of bloom they had ever shown. Next question please.'

What I did not add was that unpruned the next year too the display would have been far less and as long as the bushes were left unpruned they would deteriorate into plants of long straggling branches with an odd flower or two at the tops. In time these would gradually weaken and die back; some of them to be replaced by new shoots from the base, but these replacements would become fewer and fewer. There is no need for me to continue: most people are familar with what the rose bushes look like in a derelict garden.

In our gardens we want shapely bushes giving plenty of flowers or, if our taste lies that way, fewer blooms but of perfect quality: we shall not want old and dead twiggy growth at the base preventing the plant from sending up new vital shoots. Quite simple in itself; simple to attain, yet so often the cause of much worry — it was to me — to those beginning to grow roses. In fact some of us believe that there has been too much pre-occupation with pruning and we welcome the more liberal ideas which have been advanced in recent years.

For the job of pruning we shall need common sense, courage, stout gloves, secateurs and perhaps a pruning saw. The common sense is taken for granted. We are to carve out, as in sculpture, a shapely bush or standard, cup shaped and clear of stems inside so that, as the old Scotch gardeners have it, a bird could fly through — which is another way of saying 'let in the light and allow the air to circulate freely'. The courage will be called for in bringing oneself to make a start with the first cut. I still hang back when faced with a rose bush in the very common condition shown in Plate 73: but once the first cut has been made the rest seems easy. Courage may also be necessary to bring oneself to cut away so much of your plant — not, let me add, that I am going to enjoin on you ruthless pruning.

I have yet to solve the problem of gloves: if too stout they are clumsy, if too thin the thorns get in, or at best impede one by catching in the material; while if one has many roses to prune gauntlets are almost essential unless lacerated wrists do not matter and such gloves are expensive.

Secateurs have been prescribed: pruning knives are for the professional or for the amateur the ball of whose thumb is as tough as sole leather. There are various kinds of secateurs available and at all sorts of prices. Because of a preference for a slicing cut I have always used Wilkinson's pruners, but for cutting right down at the base of the plant where growth is thick the shape of the Rolcut can be more effective, so when pruning I carry both. A secateur with a similar type of cutting action to the Wilkinson is the Swiss Felco, which I understand is favoured for nursery use, but I have no personal experience of it. Whatever kind of secateur one goes in for it is well to keep in mind that the best quality is usually the cheapest in the long run.

In all pruning the cut should always be at an incline following the direction in which the bud is pointing — Plate 78 illustrates this. In the left hand stem in Plate 65 the cut about to be made is in the *wrong* direction. The cut is, of course, above the eye and should be $\frac{1}{4}$ in. from it. The cut in Plate 78 is right.

NEW TREES

On the footing that standards are but bush roses on a tall stock, what follows applies equally to standards.

Hybrid teas and floribundas. Pruning is to keep the bush rose in good shape, to get rid of old and dead growth and to encourage new growth. The need to build up a good structure from the beginning is why the new trees ('maidens') should be pruned back to about six inches from the base (i.e., the union). This will usually mean that three or four 'buds' are left, the top one of which should be pointing outwards. This top outward-pointing bud is really important and if necessary one must go above or below six inches to get it. Faced with a choice I tend to go below rather than above. If the new plant contains any twiggy stems they should be cut right away, so that one will usually end up with a bush consisting of two, perhaps three, and sometimes four stems about six inches long (Plate 66).

This first-year pruning is usually done in the early spring but if one is planting them out at that time it is done before planting — and a great boon it is to those of us who do not take kindly to stooping. Plates 64 to 66 show first year pruning prior to spring planting, but the same principles apply when dealing with the autumn planted bushes and standards.

Climbers of all kinds. Do *not* prune: simply cut back the tip of each shoot a few inches to a bud.

ESTABLISHED TREES

This term refers to those in their second and subsequent years. Such trees are sometimes referred to as 'cut-backs'.

With hybrid teas the first operation is to cut dead, weak and twiggy growth. In judging the last two I take the thickness of an ordinary pencil as a guide, unless of course none of the stems measure up to that standard. The remaining stems are then pruned back to an outward-pointing bud about halfway down, Plates 73 to 75. As time goes on, however, it is a good thing to cut back drastically, i.e. *hard prune*, some of the older stems, so as to get fresh growth from the base. Unless this is done the bush gets progressively taller and thinner. This halfway cutting back is known as *moderate pruning*. Some varieties, such as Peace and Eden Rose, respond better to *light pruning*, in which the stem is cut back to the first or second bud below the stalks which carried flowers in the previous year. But an occasional cutting back of the older growths should be made to get new growth from the base. The ordinary run of hybrid teas, bush or standard, usually respond best to moderate pruning. In general it can be said that the lighter the soil the less should be the pruning. Plates 76 to 77 show a bush being lightly pruned: the bush on the right in each plate has been moderately pruned. Such pruning is also shown in Plates 85 to 87. The maiden plant in Plate 66 illustrates modern ideas of hard pruning and Plate 89 shows very hard pruning.

For the **Floribundas** a combination of light and harder pruning seems to be best in order to get a long flowering period and new growth at the same time. The technique is simpler in practice than in writing. In the second year the new growth produced in the first year as a maiden is pruned lightly, that is to say, just under the stalks of the old trusses. The original stems, i.e., those which were first pruned after or on planting, will usually have sent up vigorous shoots and these should be subjected to moderate pruning, that is, cut back to a bud halfway down their length.

In the following years the process continues, namely to cut back the previous year's growth lightly and the older wood moderately. If, however, the bush is sending up vigorous new growth from its base, then the treatment of the older wood can be naturally lighter. More-over, in this way, or by leaving over the moderate pruning of the older wood for a year, quite a tall specimen floribunda shrub can be achieved.

Before leaving the pruning of hybrid teas and floribundas to deal with the climbers, there is a consequence of pruning which sometimes happens and must be mentioned. A pruning cut should produce one shoot only. Some varieties, however, tend to throw out two or three shoots, either owing to frost or other weather vagaries or because of a natural tendency. Whenever seen, these multiple shoots ought, as Plates 78 and 79 show, to be reduced to one, the biggest and healthiest looking one being kept (Plate 78) — in a trio this is usually the centre one. The next series of Plates show what happened to a vigorous flori-bunda, Faust, where a trio such as that in Plate 80 was not reduced to one shoot in its early stage nor, failing this, in the next year by reducing the three resultant stems to two by taking out the middle one (Plate 81). It will be seen that further shoots came and a real tangle developed (Plate 82). The reduction of shoot treatment was applied — Plate 83 — but as it looked rather ugly and rather too much bark was removed, more drastic treatment was given (Plate 84). This plate also gives an illustration of the cutting back of the older growth to induce new shoots (and also of the size of growth which will usually need a small pruning saw). It should be added that for this reason and to keep the bush in proper balance the stem on the left-hand side in Plate 84 was reduced to a third of the length shown in the plate.

If the pruning of **Climbers** seems somewhat complicated it is after all only a reflection of the complication of their varieties as discussed in Chapter VII. The classification made there will be some help, but there will be exceptions.

Ramblers. Taking first the *Ramblers* (Wichuraiana and the like) which include, of those mentioned in Chapter VII, Albertine, New Dawn, Emily Gray, Chaplin's Pink, American Pillar and Dorothy Perkins, the treatment is to cut away all the growth which has carried flowers. In most cases the new growth will be coming from the old stems, so that care is necessary not to cut the old growth below the new. Sometimes, however, it will be found than an old stem and its new growth will have got so badly out of hand that it is better to cut it right back to an eye about 18 in. from the base so as to encourage a new break. This cutting back should, of course, also be done to old wood generally from which no new shoots have come.

As usual there are exceptions: Dorothy Perkins and others related to her invariably throw up their new wood from the very base of the plant and not from the old wood at all. It follows, therefore, that in this type the old wood which has flowered should be cut right back to the base.

Other climbers — large flowered and so on — should be allowed to get on with it, pruning being confined to keeping these on walls, fences, etc., within the space required of them, taking out old and weak shoots, while the laterals coming out of the main stems should be kept cut back to one or two eyes (see Plate 25).

The 'pillar' types, including the Kordesii varieties, will be less vigorous and should need little more than the removal of the old and weakened wood.

Mermaid needs no pruning attention at all, unless it is getting out of hand.

SHRUBS

The shrubs are easy. Prune as judgement suggests for shape and balanced growth and get rid of any dead wood.

TIME TO PRUNE

When should they be pruned? On the whole there is general agreement that the ramblers and climbers can be disposed of in the autumn. But the others. 'Last week in March to first week in April and somewhat later in the North'. This or something like it was the generally accepted time for pruning roses.

There is no doubt that in recent years ideas have been changing and much has been heard about autumn pruning in, say, November, or at any time thereafter, the starting date being fixed by the time at which the bushes have dropped their leaves — another way of saying that the sap has ceased to flow and the tree to grow. There is nothing new in this: its pros and cons were all fully discussed in William Paul's *The Rose Garden* in 1848.

As a strictly week-end gardener I was attracted to the idea of early pruning some five years ago, not only on that account but because I hoped for earlier blooms. (Why is it we gardeners are always seeking to beat the seasons?)

One of the objections urged against early pruning is that the plant will be excited into early growth which will be killed or damaged by frosts and cold winds. On the contrary side it is held that owing to the gradual growth the shoots build up a resistance against frost and cold winds. Also, it went against the grain and common sense to be cutting off masses of new growth which March pruning so frequently entailed. Plate 85 shows some bushes of a hybrid tea in the last week of March, 1961, following moderate pruning early in the previous January. Another batch of the same variety is shown in Plate 86, just before they were similarly pruned at the end of March. The loss of new growth foliage shown in Plate 87 is striking. Incidentally the January-pruned batch finished the season nearly 12 in. higher than the March-pruned.

Be all this as it may, the worst that can happen from early pruning is that the cold will damage an incipient shoot and nature will react by producing, as already mentioned, two or three new shoots. This means the bother of rubbing out. I am not satisfied, however, that these unwanted leaf buds are solely due to cold conditions. April and May in 1960 were mild to a degree in my part of the country and yet they produced an extraordinarily large crop of this phenomenon.

In recent years, therefore, I have begun to prune well before Christmas, aiming to finish in mid-January. Until 1960 I was no keeper of records, save that, as a matter of interest, I have noted the

dates of the earliest blooms in my old garden — which were invariably those of Hugh Dickson and Marcel Gret:

	1955	1956	1957	1958
HUGH DICKSON	June 2	May 30	May 4	May 31
MARCEL GRET	June 5	June 10	May 11	June 7

There are two comments. First, the quite exceptionally sunny spring
of 1957, both north and south, will be remembered. Secondly,
there are very many more weeks between the pruning date (mid-
January at latest) and the first blooms than the thirteen usually supposed to elapse between these happenings. Of course, that figure
really relates to the growing season and whatever else December and
January may be they do not normally fall within that description. In
this connection I quote from the records kept by my friend Mr F. A.
Gibson (so often Amateur Champion at the National Rose Society
shows) of Formby, Lancs., taking Ena Harkness as an example:

	1956	1957	1958	1959
Pruned	March 18	March 2	March 8	March 8
1st bloom	June 11	June 1	June 16	May 29
No. of weeks	13	13	14	12

These results show the nearly constant pattern of 13 weeks, but more
particularly they also show the effect of that excellent 1957 spring and
the not-so-good one of 1958.

I have no 'first bloom' record for 1959 owing to the removal to a
new garden, when in consequence planting did not begin until the end
of March. In 1960, owing to a heavy planting programme, pruning
did not begin until January 16 but the bulk of it was completed by
February 21. In the result Hugh Dicksons (transferred from the old
garden) were first out on May 15 (pruned February 27) and they were
joined by Piccadilly and Sutters Gold (pruned January 16); Marcel
Gret (transferred but perhaps less favourably placed and pruned
February 22), appeared on May 25.

In general very full records were kept in 1960 and the following is
from a random sampling:

Of eleven varieties pruned between January 16 and 30, two bloomed
by May 15, seven by May 31, and eleven by June 4.

Of twenty-four varieties pruned between February 6 and 28, four bloomed by May 15, twenty-two by May 31, and twenty-four by June 4.

Of nine varieties pruned between March 5 and April 2, five bloomed by June 8, and nine by June 17.

Although the more detailed records relate to one year only and should not therefore be regarded as conclusive, I think the general picture from what has been said is that whatever the pruning date may be the spring weather will be the deciding factor as to the dates of blooming. Secondly, that pruning earlier than February will not produce any earlier blooms, and there may be disadvantages.

There are, however, two other aspects in favour of doing one's pruning before February. One is that the experts enjoin us to cut back early in the autumn the long growth in order to limit the effects of high winds (page 173): why then make two bites? The other and weightier one is to remind oneself of the numerous other garden operations which, according to the diaries, have to be done in February, and the more so in March.

XIX

Pests and Diseases

A READER can usually judge when a writer is enjoying his writing —
whatever the reader may be feeling. This is a chapter that I do not
like, not because I lack experience of the subject — the reverse is true
as regards diseases — but because a catalogue of what can happen to
roses is liable to give the impression that they have more troubles than
other flowering plants and are therefore difficult to grow well. That they
are liable to diseases and pests is perfectly true: so are children — well,
at any rate to diseases — but they do not all suffer nor do all those
that do, die. Moreover, the liability of children to diseases does not
noticeably put people off having them. So let us, expecting the best,
prepare for the worst — which in the event is normally not very
terrible.

PESTS

In writing about pests I have had to check an urge to write too much,
because attendance at nature study classes has given me a mine of not
entirely useful, but certainly delightful information on them. The
little I allow myself to say, as it were off-beam, may make the little
beasts that attack roses a trifle more interesting. Nevertheless they
have to be disposed of.

For the most part the rose pests seem to be more in evidence in
the early spring than in the summer. 'A' is for **Aphides,** or for
most of us plain **Greenfly** (although some aphides are black). In their
sphere they are the harbingers of spring, having been waiting for it
since their eggs were laid in the previous autumn on the woody
parts of bushes. There are only about 450 species of aphides. Their
power and speed of reproduction make rabbits appear to be positively
sterile and their method of feeding is fascinating. They dig most dili-
gently into the young leaflets, usually on the underside, and into the
tiny buds. Once dug in they steadily suck up the sap until for lack of it

the growth shrivels up and dies off — or is malformed, Plate 88). During the feeding process the greenfly exudes excess sugar, known as 'honeydew', and this forms the sticky substance one finds on the plants attacked. Greenfly have the capacity when dead to give birth to their young: so do not think your spraying is ineffective if very soon after the brutes are back again.

Fortunately birds, such as the tits, delight in them: so do not be worried if you see birds on your rose bushes, apparently pecking at the young buds. The larvae of the ladybirds love them too, so do not destroy these rather evil-looking larvae. But the chap for my money is the ichneumon fly which lances through the skin of the greenfly to lay eggs inside it. In due course the resulting larvae feed on their host. Unfortunately, I do not know how to breed or to attract ichneumon flies.

However, with only a few roses bushes quite the best way to assist the ichneumon flies and others in their good purpose, and they usually do need assistance, is some good plain finger-and-thumb work — the thing is to squash the aphides and not the young shoots and buds. This treatment can also be recommended for another set of early arrivals, usually in May — the **Caterpillars** or, more technically, the larvae of various moths. Left unchecked the caterpillar will eat the leaves, sometimes 'mining' into them and producing a skeleton leaf. Equally they damage the young buds which are either destroyed or produce malformed flowers. A caterpillar hanging on a silken thread is fairly obvious, unless perhaps its colour matches that of the foliage, but beware the rolled up or rolled down leaf. It almost invariably houses — and very safely from sprays and powders too — the grub of one of the many species of the sawfly or the caterpillar of the tortrix moth.

Thrips also arrive early. They would, no doubt, also yield to finger and thumb work could one but see them. The damage they do is clearly visible in ruined buds and flowers — the tip of the bud looks as if it has been chewed off — and in the markings they make on leaves. But I never see a thrip itself. This is hardly surprising as they measure only 1/20 in. long. A knowledgeable friend once broke open an affected bud and, pointing to some minute specks, said 'Thrips'. True, but premature: they were the eggs which the insect deposits inside a bud as soon as the outer covering has begun to open.

Frog Hopper. Nor have I seen a frog hopper hop. Under the name of **Cuckoo Spit** it is that well known mass of frothy spittle, usually to be seen between the axils of the leaves and the stem, inside of which is a yellowish green nymph — in due course this becomes the hopper itself. The nymph enjoys the same kind of food as the aphis and can be finger and thumbed too.

Rose Leaf Hopper. This is another kind of hopper — the rose leaf hopper — which I have never seen in action. It operates in the same way as that of the frog hopper and the result of its withdrawing sap from the leaves is to give them a mottled appearance.

Capsid Bug. If some of your rose leaves and buds have a brownish appearance it may be due to the capsid bug. I have never seen it or its damage. It is interested in other vegetation besides roses.

Ants are a common nuisance in the garden and they are very partial to the sugar excretion of the aphides; both insects are often seen on the roses at the same time. In this respect they are harmless, but in the fabrication of their nests they can remove — with detrimental effect — practically all the soil from the roots of a rose plant. This I have suffered from. They are said to transport aphides from one rose bush to another: I await a sight of this with interest.

Leaf-Cutting Bee. A pest I have seen, and also its damage, is the leaf-cutting bee. It does this with such efficient smoothness and for such a good purpose that I have quite an affection for it. With great precision it cuts out circular and sausage-shaped pieces from the edge of the rose leaves. With the latter pieces it lines the walls of a tunnel-like cell (about the size and shape of a fountain pen top), in which it lays its eggs, placing a circular piece of leaf between each egg and the next. The only ways I have seen suggested for coping with this bee is to net it in flight or when on a rose bush, or to destroy its nest. I am glad to know that the nest is extremely difficult to find, whether it be in the ground, an old tree stump or a wall. Fortunately, too, growing good roses does not depend on chasing leaf-cutting bees with a bee net.

INSECTICIDES

Where the use of finger and thumb is inappropriate, repulsive or too irksome there are a wide variety of liquid sprays and dusts available.

There is the ubiquitous but undiscriminating DDT obtainable as a dust or as a spray, but it is quite useless against greenfly. Indeed, it is a menace because it will put the ladybirds and ichneumon flies out of action and also my pet the leaf-cutting bee. Then there are the more lately developed controls such as lindane and malathion. There are, too, what are known as systemic poisons, based on the fact that a plant can absorb them through the roots, pass them into the foliage and buds and so provide a Borgia-like feast for the pests.

For convenience there are set out below the remedies usually recommended against the chief pests of the rose and what it is said they will deal with. In considering them it is useful, when the number of roses is relatively small, to keep in mind the utility of the aerosol packs. With these, remember to follow the instructions, and not to direct the spray directly at the leaves.

Lindane	*D D T*	*Malathion*
Aphides	Caterpillars	Aphides
Capsids	Thrips	Leaf Hoppers
Thrips	Leaf Hoppers	Leaf Miners
Leaf Hoppers	Capsids	Thrips
Leaf Miners	Sawflies	
Ants		

I have used lindane and malathion, within their ranges, with equally good effect.

DISEASES

Black Spot, Botrytis or Grey Mould, Chlorosis, Crown Gall, Downy Mildew, Rust, Leaf Scorch, Powdery Mildew, Rose Anthracnose, Sooty Mould, Stem Canker and more. Those who know Jerome's *Three Men in a Boat* will also know what happened to that writer when he foolishly read a medical encyclopaedia. He found that he had every disease under the sun, except housemaid's knee — which, by the way, shows that Jerome was no gardener. To save rose growers from the same fate, I deal only, but pretty extensively, with the three main diseases, leaving the others, and you, to get on with it. No doubt, if my roses had suffered from any of the others I should not be so off-hand. But it is not as bad as that: of those in the list Sooty Mould is the result of not attending to the aphides and their honeydew (p. 158): Chlorosis is not precisely a disease but a symptom of nutritional deficiencies (page 165); while for the remainder there is no really effective cure so, as the infected tree or foliage will die anyway, it seems best for us to adopt the doctor's advice to Jerome — 'not to stuff up his head with things he did not understand'. Mildew (powdery), Rust and Black Spot, however, must be faced. They are all known as fungus diseases.

98. *A group of hybrid musks, including Felicia, Penelope and Will Scarlet, kept pruned back for ordinary bedding purposes. Allowed to grow freely the hybrid musks make good hedges and specimen shrubs. This group can also be seen in Plate 32 (bottom right).*

99. *Purple spotting* (left); *black spot* (middle, two examples); *rust and black spot* (top right); *mildew* (bottom right).

100. '*And the fruits thereof*' — *the large and tomato-like heps of the rugosa shrub rose Scabrosa. They follow on from the large, single, deep mauve-pink flowers. The foliage of this group is an attractive feature.*

Mildew. This is the commonest disease, the easiest to recognize, responds well to preventive treatment and, taken early, can be cured without causing serious damage.

Plate 99 shows what it looks like — a white powder covering the surface of buds, stems and leaves. But with experience one gets to know that a plant is infected before the white powder appears. The foliage crinkles and curves and looks rather unhappy, purple patches appear and then the powder. Early treatment is clearly to be preferred rather than late. One tends to associate mildew with damp cellars and the like but general humidity as such does not produce rose mildew. Ideal conditions for the spores of the fungus are hottish days followed by cold or cool nights plus their usual accompaniment — heavy dews. The conditions in 1959 were ideal. The rôle of the dew, which is, of course, a light dusting of moisture, is to enable the spores to get a hold on the plant. Heavy moisture, such as rain, however, puts up a positive barrier against the spores adhering.

Like the rain, the dew and the spores fall on the just and unjust without distinction, but there are many rose varieties which can resist attack without aid. On the other hand, less resistant varieties can be quite irregular in contracting the disease. I had a hedge of three dozen Frensham which used to get it on exactly the same three adjacent bushes each year while the remainder kept entirely free. This may have been due to root dryness at the particular spot, but for quite a while I put it down to draughty conditions. This I now doubt because mildew seems to thrive in the enclosed and closely confined gardens of London and other large towns. The susceptibility of certain varieties to the disease has been mentioned in the earlier chapters but unless a variety is a complete martyr I would never avoid growing it on that account only.

Colloidal copper white oil emulsion is a well established spraying treatment both for prevention and cure. Karathane, a more recent introduction, is favoured by some people, especially as the colloidal copper white oil is not compatible with some of the other spraying compounds (page 167). Karathane is also obtainable as a dust which can be convenient when one has only a few bushes for treatment. Other proprietary rose mildew specifics are offered.

Rust. If, on looking at the back of your rose leaves, you find rusty orange coloured swellings — pustules is the correct description — then it is pretty certain to be rust. It is shown in Plate 99. One experience of the disease is described on page 66, when I lost a bed of Fashion.

L

The other came from Conrad F. Meyer described on page 83.

Fatal results from rust are common, but an attack detected in its earliest stage may be mitigated if the infected leaves, whether on the plant or on the ground, are cleared away at once. But I am afraid that on the whole rust must be regarded as a killer, if not directly, then by so weakening the plant that it becomes an easy victim to the effects of severe weather and of other diseases. We can take heart, however, from the experts who suggest that we need not fear attacks every year, as it seems to come in cycles and especially in areas subject to heavy dews. Obviously if one is in a rust-prone neighbourhood, such as south west England, susceptible varieties should be avoided.

Fashion has already been mentioned: the hybrid tea, Hector Deane, is under suspicion, so is Crimson Glory, but both have been quite free with me. The Queen, offered in some catalogues, can certainly contract it.

There is no certain preventive of rose rust, or cure for it. In any event its local incidence and cyclic appearance indicates that general preventive spraying is unnecessary and all one can suggest is wholesale spraying of one's roses with a thiram compound the moment one sees the pustules appearing.

Black Spot. Mildew is a nuisance and rust a killer, black spot lies between. It looks like an ink spot and much ink has been used in the past writing about it and, I dare say, will be used in the future. There is no cure yet and no 100 per cent effective preventive. But all is not gloom. Rose growers in most of the industrial areas of this country have never seen those ink spots because the chemicals in the air prevent the spores from infecting the rose foliage. The growers in the country know all about it, especially those in the West Country and in Sussex, where the conditions seem particularly propitious for severe attacks.

The spores of the disease are carried by the wind and, it is said, by splashing rain on to the rose foliage. Here they send out colourless threads which penetrate the outer skin of the leaf and enter the cells immediately below. It is these threads which cause the cells to degenerate and produce the black spot with its typical fringed edge. The spots are really brown and when numerous they overlap and form large areas. Infection usually begins on the lower and, therefore, maturer leaves and spreads gradually, but sometimes quite rapidly, throughout the plant. Eventually the infected leaves assume yellowish tones and then drop off and sometimes the whole plant can be completely defoliated. The stems can be infected too, and as a result they may die back during the winter. Plate 90. Following defoliation the plant will endeavour to produce another crop of foliage from the leaf buds, which in the ordinary way would not grow out until the following year. This double production of foliage in one year is at the expense of weakening the plant and so making it less resistant to attack in the next year.

The spores need both time and the right conditions to make themselves felt. One often reads that black spot does not appear before July or, in a gardening calendar, that spraying against it should begin in that month. Actually the spores begin to get on to the new growth as soon as it appears, but they take time to develop and for the threads to get through the skin of the leaf and then for the spots to appear.

A damp atmosphere with the temperature around 70° is said to be ideal and as these conditions are usually *fully* established in July, hence the reference to that month. But the spores remain active in infected leaves until they disintegrate completely, and on the stems. A mild winter means undropped and undecayed foliage and a flying start for the disease on any warm and damp spring days. Personally, I look for black spot from the moment my plants produce foliage.

Once the threads are through the skin they are untouchable and nothing can prevent the black spots appearing, nor can anything be done to take them away. That is why there is no cure. There is only protection. This is directed to killing off the overwintering spores before they get moving in the spring and, more particularly, sealing the surface of the new growth against the entry of the threads. Ladies will get the idea of this from their use of barrier creams. It is this which lies behind the recommendation to spray against black spot immediately after pruning and when the young shoots begin to appear. Thereafter spraying at regular intervals, 10 to 14 days, from the end of June to September, is suggested. In my black spot paradise I am not content with this, and having given the young shoots a first shot I continue with three more at 14-day intervals; this normally takes one to the end of May. If any black spot does appear then spraying recommences and continues at 7-day intervals.

There is a preventive measure with which I have little patience. It is to pick up and destroy all the fallen leaves. ·Whenever I read it I wonder whether those who recommend it carry out their own advice. If you have tried to do it properly, even on one small bed of say, a dozen roses, you will know exactly what I mean. Regarding this, according to research at the Agricultural Research Center, Baltsville, Maryland, U.S.A., neither winter treatment by such things as lime sulphur, organic mercury fungicides nor clean culture, i.e., leaf removal, has any effect on the subsequent incidence of black spot. This research also claims to have found that one of the most effective treatments was to prune the roses down to within 1 or 2 in. of the bud union, Plate 89. It is claimed that this severe treatment had no ultimate effect on the flowers, but naturally they came later than usual.*

I am bound to say that this does seem to answer a question which the leaf pickers-up leave unposed and unanswered: what about the spores overwintering in the stems? I tried a test on these lines with two varieties prone to black spot in 1960 but the result was inconclusive — all I am prepared to say just now is that there *may* be something in it.

The colloidal copper white oil emulsion, already mentioned, is still a favoured spray against black spot, but other chemicals are in use, partly because they are considered to be more effective and partly because of the question of compatibility. Captan is one which is now used extensively. Another product is zineb. A later product, and one which has attracted much attention in the U.S.A., is maneb. Captan is also available as a dust.

The only agreeable feature I know about black spot is that sometimes it is not. Before one has seen black spot in the flesh, as it were, there is often the chance that it will be confused with a purple spotting or blotching on rose foliage. This is a condition quite unrelated to black spot. If the black-spotted leaves in the middle of Plate 99 are compared with the leaves on the left the difference will be readily apparent. The purple spotting is seldom circular, the spots are smaller and, more important, the fringed edge is absent.

I gather that there are several types of purple spotting — they all seem the same to me — and many explanations of their cause are put forward. The most frequently offered is unbalanced soil and feeding. Some varieties are said to be more susceptible than others. Hugh Dickson is one, but it seems to suffer just as much in the fertile soil of my new garden as it did in the thin stuff of the old one. Purple spotting can, it is said, make the leaves drop earlier, but it produces none of that complete collapse of individual leaves nor the complete defoliation which is so characteristic of black spot. But the experts say that it will behave like black spot if it is treated with a black spot spray: it never has with me.

* *Horticultural Abstracts* 29–750.

101. *This is not the truss of a floribunda, but the 'chandelier' of buds produced by some hybrid teas, especially in the autumn.* 102. *Left alone there will be a mass of small blooms and most people will disbud. But it should be done earlier than shown here — when the buds are about pea size.*

103. Hole made by leaving tall growers to rock in autumn winds. If subsequently filled with ice the results can be fatal. 104. A sucker at the base of a standard with soil removed to facilitate removal. 105. — which is done by cutting it off right back to the stock.

In these days we seem far from the simple soapy water with which in my boyhood I used to spray the standard roses. Never were there so many gardening aids available — the thing is to find one's way about, especially when gossip and the news tells of yet another and more effective fungicide or insect killer. We gardeners must remember, however, that specifics of this kind may be excellent for commercial use, that is on farm and nursery, where proper precautions against harm to the workers and to other crops can be taken, but they can be a real danger in the garden. This is why the latest specific we may hear about does not seem to become available to us. In this connection may I commend the *List of Approved Products* (1962 Edition), under the Agricultural Chemicals Approval Scheme, published by the Ministry of Agriculture, Fisheries and Food. It may be had free of charge from the Ministry. Primarily put out for the commercial grower, it has particular value for the gardener in that it shows what products are available in retail packs for use by amateur gardeners. Those who read it will also be able to see why so many products are not made available in this way.

Finally and most important, whatever product is used in the garden against diseases, always carry out the maker's directions and cautions.

NUTRITIONAL DEFICIENCES

Nutritional deficiences come in aptly at this point because their symptoms may be thought to indicate that the plant is diseased and because a strong healthy plant is much more likely to recover from a severe attack of disease than a weakly one. Advisedly I do not say 'is more likely to be immune from attack'.

The deficiencies are not always easy to identify. If your rose plants are stunted with thin shoots, small in size and number with pale green leaves which tend to fall off, and there are few blooms, it may be suffering from a lack of nitrogen. But thin small shoots, lack of flowers and falling leaves may also mean that phosphates are needed: the distinction being that in the case of the latter the leaves do not yellow but tend to come dull green with a reddish tint. Moreover, the flower buds may never get beyond that stage. However, if one wants to be absolutely certain whether it is phosphate deficiency one is advised to dig up the plant and see whether it has extremely poorly developed roots. Does one put the plant back afterwards? Fortunately this deficiency is far from common.

Leaves browned or scorched on the edges and bluish green in colour or yellowing between the veins may mean insufficient potash. On the other hand the browning and scorching may well mean those dratted cold north-east winds in March following on mild and, therefore, growing weather.

Yellowing of the leaves is commonly called 'chlorosis' and is seen at its best, or worst, when there is an iron or magnesium deficiency. In the latter case the older leaves pale first; in the former it is the young leaves at the ends of the shoots which first show the symptom, which gradually extends to the older ones. In both kinds of deficiency the leaves gradually shrivel and fall off. The lack of iron is the more likely in alkaline soils, which, of course, includes chalk.

The remedies are clear, namely, to give the plant what it appears to lack. Here foliar feeding is useful as the best results are said to be obtained by spraying on the appropriate chemical. For example, a solution of $\frac{1}{2}$ oz. of potassium nitrate to a gallon of water, plus a spreader, will act against a nitrogen deficiency. Iron and manganese are best conveyed, according to the National Rose Society, by means of sequestrenes, which can be purchased from sundriesmen.

All the foregoing about nutritional deficiencies is based on the experience of other and wiser people, as my roses do not seem to have suffered in this way. Occasionally in the late spring a few bushes may have shown the signs of chlorosis, but this, I am pretty sure, was due to lack of moisture or a local upset in the soil. Nor do I think that, given balanced feeding, the plants in the ordinary run of garden will suffer.

In short, do not worry about it. And the same applies as regards the other diseases and the pests. Like other things one is anxious about they may never happen. To this is added the suggestion that if one is beginning to grow roses, and no fellow gardener in one's neighbourhood mutters darkly about black spot and mildew, do not trouble to take precautions in the first year — see what happens and act accordingly in the future.

XX

Spraying, Cultivation and Maintenance

SPRAYING

IF one is going to spray, either from inclination or necessity, it is better to do the job properly and also with the minimum amount of labour. The busy gardener will not want to spray against aphids one evening, caterpillars the next, then against mildew, followed by another operation for black spot. He will seek to combine the sprays into one operation. Thus currently my spraying solution consists of malathion against the chief pests, Karathane against mildew, zineb against black spot, a dose of a foliar feed and a wetting agent. For some years an antibiotic was added as it was said to increase the resistance of roses to mildew. It may have done, but I did not notice it. By the way, antibiotics are not generally available for horticultural purposes.

This witch's brew can, of course, be varied: lindane being substituted for the malathion or the better-known captan taking the place of zineb. What cannot be allowed is to have, for instance, a foliar feed in the same mixture as a colloidal copper fungicide (against mildew or black spot). Similarly the latter must not be mixed with some of the rose mildew specifics.

This question of compatibility is most important as the wrong mixture can have fatal results on the rose foliage. Some manufacturers and distributors put out most useful information as to the extent of the compatibility of their products: others do not. The need to get information on this score before mixing a particular specific with others cannot be over emphasized. Nor, once again, can be the need to keep strictly to the maker's directions when mixing sprays, either alone or with others.

As to quantities, I hope that I am not being too elementary by mentioning that if, for example, one is using a mixture of, say, two ingredients both of which are directed to be dissolved in two gallons of water, one does not need four gallons. On the other hand, if the directions for one are a teaspoonful to two gallons and for the other a teaspoonful to one gallon, then two teaspoonfuls of the latter will be necessary.

Time of day to spray. For most gardeners the best period of the day to carry out spraying will be the time at which we can do it and this usually means the evening. This is good enough: the thing to avoid is when the sun is full, because then the drops of solution will magnify the sun's rays to an extent that foliage will be scorched. I have always understood, however, that the most effective time — especially for foliar feeling — is early morning as soon as daylight appears. As to this may I say to those who have not seen their gardens — no matter how small — and particularly their roses glistening in the early morning dew have missed moments of unbelievable beauty and of much contentment. Then you will see not only the roses, but what Sergeant Cuff thought were so much less worthy to be looked at — diamonds too.

Sprayers. Other than digging up some newly planted climbing hops to see how they were getting on my earliest gardening operation was the spraying of the standard roses already mentioned. 'Syringing' would be the more correct description, because one used a fairly large cylindrical instrument, with about twenty pin holes at the end, producing a short and sharp, but forceful, burst of liquid. Most efficacious against the cuckoo spit, passing boys and, followed by profound apologies, adults. But hardly in line with modern ideas. These are in favour of producing a very fine mist, with force in it too — near the nozzle.

There are all kinds of sprayers available which operate in this way. They range from much improved types of the old syringe, including one producing a continuous spray by opening and shutting the sprayer like a telescope, to small and not so small pneumatic machines. One's choice will depend on how much spraying is necessary, one's pocket, and to some extent one's physical capacity, as the pneumatic sprayers have to be pumped up, although the latest models make provision for a special nozzle for using a motor car tyre foot pump. As a measure of what may be needed my experience is that one gallon of spraying solution will cover satisfactorily up to a hundred bushes when in full foliage.

For nearly ten years I have used with satisfaction, and still use, a Mysto pneumatic sprayer having a total capacity of three gallons, that is, two gallons of spray and one gallon volume of compressed air. Full it is heavy, but it can be comfortably carried by the pumping handle and put down every few yards. I graduated to this *via* a small hand pneumatic sprayer, rather like a blow-lamp in shape, but the capacity was really too small even for a few roses. Since I purchased my Mysto, improved models have become available, with working capacities of one, two or three gallons and of lighter weight. I am using one of the smallest for distant parts of the rose garden and I am quite satisfied with it. I have also used a sprayer in which the pressure is obtained through an air compressor operated by my electric drill: this, of course, eliminates any kind of physical pumping. A not unimportant advantage of working with a pneumatic sprayer is that it allows the busy gardener to study and enjoy his individual bushes, which the distractions of hand operation tend to prevent.

Spraying materials are not so cheap that one can afford to waste them: gardening time is also valuable. Thus in carrying out a course of preventive spraying treatment there is little sense and positive waste in abandoning it part way through. As to the amount of spray to be used, it is not necessary to have the rose bush positively dripping with the solution: it will have had sufficient as soon as drops begin to fall off the foliage. But see that the stems get their share and remember that it is important to spray both surfaces of the leaves. Particularly in connection with black spot, get right into the centre of the plant and give special attention to the lower foliage — see Plates 91 and 92. By the way, American research holds that the frequency and thoroughness of spraying is more important than choice of preparation.*

Fungicides like Karathane and Captan are not dissolved in the water but are suspended in it. There is therefore a tendency after the initial mixing for it to sink gradually to the bottom of the container. This means not only an uneven mixture but, as the solution gets lower, it tends to thicken and choking of the nozzle of the sprayer can occur. An occasional agitation of the container is therefore useful.

CULTIVATION AND MAINTENANCE

If roses are what they are claimed to be this should be a short section. It will, however, cover a long period of time, though not all that amount of work. The order followed is roughly that of the sequence

*Ohio Farm House Research: *Horticultural Abstracts* 30–1062

of events which normally follow on after pruning — it being assumed that meat and bone meal or bone meal or fish manure or a proprietary organic manure has been pricked into the beds as suggested in Chapter XVI or in accordance with the maker's directions as the case may be.

Naturally you will be watching with special interest the growth on the newly planted roses. It may be found that among them there are one or two which seem to be lagging behind and show no sign of 'breaking'. Do not think they are on their way out. Instead firm down the soil around the base and give the plant a couple of gallons of water, and all should be well.

Mulching. Come May one has to think about *mulching*. By that month the soil should have warmed up in the spring sunshine. Mulching while the soil is cold will keep it cold. For the lucky few the mulch can be a dressing of farmyard manure, but for most of us other material must suffice. The mulch can also be combined, with the spring dose of fertilizer. If, for instance, one is using peat as a mulch, fertilizer can be mixed with it at the rate of 4 oz. to 1½ lb. and spread at the rate of 2 lb. to the square yard. But there are the other humus makers mentioned in Chapter XV available, such as spent hops, compost and so on.

Be sure, however, that the compost is in fact fully mature. You will rue the day if the mixture is immature and therefore containing un-decayed grass and live seeds — look at Plate 93. Or you may prefer the cheapest of all mulching materials — grass cuttings. Cheap in the sense that they cost nothing and cheap in labour because putting them on the rose beds will often save a longer journey to take them to the compost heap for treatment. But some discretion in their use is necessary. It is no use tipping them out in great clots from the grass box. In such heaps the grass heats up, mats up and generally does little good. They should be sprinkled and spread on to the bed — a process which can well continue so long as the grass box is on the mower.

You may, however, curse grass cuttings on your rose beds if they come from a weed-ridden lawn. Never shall I forget the year when, in an evil moment, I trundled into the garden barrow load after barrow load of coarse grass cuttings from the neighbouring churchyard, in order to mulch the roses. This indeed they did, but never have I seen a finer crop of daisies, buttercups and the like — just like the grass weeds shown in Plate 93. It took many week-ends to get rid of them.

Again, there is a doctor in ·Wales who has never forgiven me for a broadcast in which, when extolling the virtues of grass cuttings as a mulch, I did not give a warning that cuttings from a lawn recently treated with a hormone weedkiller can be lethal. The doctor seems to think that I owe him for thirty-eight rose bushes.

In April and May, when mulching or when admiring the splendour and variety of the colours in the spring foliage, Plate 106, one should look out for the *pruning cuts where the bud has died*. Below the dead bud there is usually a fine bud or shoot pointing inwards. If you are strong willed you will ignore it and cut back to the next outward pointing bud.

The dead bud at the end of a pruned shoot is not the same thing as the *blind shoots*, which Peace and some of its progeny are inclined to produce — the shoot and leaves are there all right but no flower bud. To get a flower bud pinch or cut back the shoot to the next leaf axil.

But more important is early treatment where the bud at the pruning cut has produced *multiple shoots*. This was described on page 152.

Disbudding. When the flower buds begin to appear — it is hardly profitable to point to any particular date as so much depends on locality, the kind of spring and to a lesser extent the date of pruning — one will have to think about *disbudding*. I know of a very small London garden, 35 ft. by 18 ft., not four miles from Charing Cross, with a good deal of shade, where the roses put up a brave show. Blooms of any size are precious and the owner would never dream of disbudding. Nor would I. Others whose gardens are more favourably situated may wish to ensure specially choice blooms and this inevitably means disbudding.

I have already indicated my own practice of reducing the buds to not more than two on a stem — leaving the topmost one and the lowest so as to get continuity of display. For really outstanding blooms one must come down to one flower bud per stem and even rub out all inward pointing leaf buds before they break. Plate 101 shows what happens when disbudding is not practised — the chandelier-like effect is very common in the autumn flush.

By the way, even if one does not practise disbudding, the chandeliers when in flower look much better without the central bloom — so perhaps this bud might be taken out. Disbudding is best done before the buds begin to drain on the plant's energy, that is, as soon as they can be handled — the size of a small pea or less if one is nimble-fingered. It may be useful to know, as an aid in deciding what buds to leave on the bush, that the average time between discernible bud and mature bloom is usually about one month.

The tendency of certain varieties, such as Rose Gaujard and Grand Gala, to produce blooms with split or muddled centres has been mentioned. It is said that there is less likelihood of this if when disbudding a side bud is retained instead of the top one. As I am not in the least worried by an occasional split bloom I cannot confirm or deny the assertion. The Grand Gala in Plate 38 has an excellent muddled centre and the Perfecta on its right has a split centre. Of course the disbudding business is directed towards the hybrid teas, not to the floribundas and the rest, although as noted in Chapter VI certain varieties of floribundas can be disbudded to produce quite sizable blooms of hybrid tea type.

Feeding and spraying. We shall be giving another dose of fertilizer in mid-June or when indicated by the maker. We shall, of course, have been coping with the greenfly and the less likely other pests. And according to our location and fears we shall be continuing the preventive spraying against black spot: while, come July, those in the prone areas will be the more keenly alerted.

Watering should not worry one. The mulching will help to conserve the moisture in the beds, but if it is felt that there must be watering then it must be done properly: sprinkling with can or hose is useless. Indeed worse than useless if there has been spraying against diseases, as sprinkling will act like rain and wash off the protective fungicides. The watering should, therefore, be at ground level. Perhaps the knowledge that each plant ought to have a gallon poured around the roots may encourage you to leave it to nature. Where really necessary, nature may have to be assisted, as suggested earlier with those climbers on the walls of the house — 3 gallons twice a week.

Hoeing. I am not going to enter into the arguments as to whether regular hoeing helps to conserve moisture. It will probably be necessary anyway on account of weeds — mulches are not absolutely weed-proof. But no deep hoeing because of those surface hair roots. On that account I have always used the Swoe, the shape of which is based on the old sproughton hoe. Its balance gives just about the right depth, 1–2 in., and its shape enables one to get comfortably behind each individual bush.

106. 'The promise of spring'. Many people can get aesthetic as well as gardening satisfaction at a sight like this, including as it does a wonderful range of colour tones and the pattern of the pruned rose trees.

107. *The end of the season — 28th November 1960.*

Blooms for the house. Naturally we shall want some and something has been said on their behaviour there in Chapter XIV. What I want to suggest here is that in cutting them from plants in their first year great restraint should be exercised. Long stalks are usually wanted, which means cutting off much foliage too, and as the foliage plays such a large part in the growth of a plant it is better not to take it away in the 'building-up' period. When one does cut, try to do it just above an outward pointing leaf.

Dead Heading. A sense of tidyness will encourage us to cut off the dead heads, but it is good gardening practice too, since if left on the plant they tend to prevent or to delay the production of new flowers. The standard in Plate 12, (taken mid-August), bloomed in mid-June 1961 and was not dead-headed — it produced a fine crop of heps but no more blooms that year.

The careful grower will also cut the dead heads off just above an outward pointing leaf. The less careful, and those of us who have much to do and little time, will simply snap off the old bloom and leave it to nature's efficient processes: the old stalk will die back to the next leaf bud, which in the meantime will have been getting on with the job of growing.

Summer Pruning. Here let us dispose of the 'mystique' called summer pruning. Like the chap who was unaware that he had been writing prose all his life, most people do not realise that in cutting blooms for the house in the way suggested, and to some extent in dead-heading, they are summer pruning. It can be left at that.

A variation on the summer pruning theme is the suggestion that new growth coming late in the summer will not ripen and owing to its sappiness it will not survive the winter. Maybe it will not, but perhaps it may and I think it better to leave it until pruning time. It is, however, only fair to give warning that although such new growth sometimes appears to have survived the winter it may collapse and die later, if not during the spring, then after the first crop of flowers. This means that if you are an early pruner you will have to go over your plants again to cut out the corpses.

I have much more sympathy with the exhortation to *cut back the taller growth in the early autumn* so as to reduce the rocking of the bush by wind. This rocking can make a sizeable hole, as Plate 103 shows. In a severe winter this hole can become filled with solid ice, with real detriment to the plant. Moreover, the rocking will damage the roots. Of course, if one decides on autumn pruning that will take the place of a separate operation to deal with rocking.

Suckers seem to loom in people's minds rather more than they need. A sucker (in rose parlance) is the result of the root stock doing some growing on its own account: it sends up a fine healthy shoot which goes on growing in the ordinary way. A good growth of suckers left undisturbed can eventually swamp and kill the rose plant proper. Suckers can come from the root stock just below the union — Plates 104 and 105 show one such and how it is removed by cutting right back to the stock — or they can come from a root quite a distance from the plant. Here one should remove the soil down to the root concerned and cut it right through *between* the sucker and the plant.

Standards will sometimes produce suckers quite high up on their main stems. One should have little difficulty in recognizing a sucker as in addition to the places where it may appear it has a somewhat fresh and healthy look and is usually a lighter tone than the foliage on the plant.

Had this book been written in 1960 instead of 1961 I should have been inclined to say that over the years I could hardly understand the fuss made about suckers, because I seldom ever had one. The experience of 1961, however, make me more cautious. Why there should be this variation I do not know: all I can do is to call attention to the last line of the introduction to this book.

PART SIX

How much they cost

A Rose Budget

XXI

A Rose Budget

WHAT a man spends on his hobbies is nobody's business any more than what his wife spends on her . . . I will not continue: there will be, I hope, too many wives reading this book. But we had better finish with some ideas about what it costs to grow roses well and, therefore, to get the maximum enjoyment from them.

Let us take 250 as the unit. But please do not think that I am advocating that other responsibilities should be disregarded and that that number should be bought at once. By all means do so if beds can be made ready and purse allows, but obviously one can build up gradually or set the target at a lower figure. And believe me, with such a number you will know your individual bushes far better and will get just as much if not more pleasure than those of us who have passed into the thousand category.

Take the largest item first — the plants. In looking at this it is well to remember that they can give practically continuous bloom from mid-June to mid-November — a somewhat shorter period in the north, and a somewhat longer one in favoured localities. With reasonable care, particularly in the preparation of the soil and in planting, they will last from 12 to 15 years at least. I suggest that in this costing exercise — based on 1961 prices — we go in for ten dozen hybrid teas and a like number of floribundas. To make up the 250 we will add six standards and four pillar roses to break up the rather flat lines of roses in beds.

Quality roses, once they are outside the novelty class, cost 5s. each or 55s. a dozen. The bush roses (20 dozen or 40 half dozens) will mean £55 and six standard at 16s. each and four pillar roses (with the necessary pillars) at 8s. each adds £6. 8s., to give a total of £61. 8s. od. Of course you can buy roses cheaper, but as already indicated I do not recommend it.

Our 250 roses will require beds totalling in area about 140 ft. by 6 ft.

i.e., nearly 100 square yards. It is approximately this area on which other calculations have been based. The cost of preparing the beds is difficult to fix. It is assumed that we shall 'do it ourselves'. The price of farm manure, if one can get it, varies considerably. The contents of the compost heap should cost nothing. If peat is used then on the basis of 40 bushels we shall need to spend about £4.

In an otherwise quite good book about rose growing there is a list under 'Tools' of no less than 22 articles. It included two cultivators, three forks, three hoes and three spades. This kind of advice is distinctly off-putting. The writer did add that preparation and maintenance could be done with many fewer tools: I should think so too. All that I have ever used are the following first-grade tools: spade and large fork, 30s. and 27s. respectively; edging iron, 21s.; border fork, 25s. The border fork is most important, and equally so is a hoe. A Dutch type in pressed steel is about 20s., but if you can spare the extra money go for the Swoe even though it is twice the price. Secateurs will be needed, good ones may vary from around 17s. 6d. to 'Rolls-Royce' types at 50s. Let us put the total for tools at £10.

To this must be added the cost of a sprayer. The price range is a wide one, but to be on the safe side let us take the cost of a good one-gallon pneumatic type as about £6.

This completes (and a good thing too) the capital expenditure: roses £61. 8s. 0d.; bed preparation material £4; tools, etc. £16, making a total of £81. 8s. 0d. This figure looks somewhat staggering, but on the conservative basis of the expenditure being good for say 12 years, it looks decidedly more reasonable at under £7 a year or 6½d. a bush.

Cost of upkeep must, however, be added to complete the financial picture. In my early days I estimated that 5 per cent of my roses would be lost annually. The loss has not reached 1 per cent, so I suggest that the cost of replacements can be ignored.

On the basis of using 12 oz. of fertilizer, of one kind or another, per square yard, and this is certainly on the right side, the approximate cost would be not more than £2. 10s. a year. To this £1. 10s. can be added for sufficient quantities of spraying materials, making £4 or just under 4d. a bush.

Add to this 4d. the 6½d. for capital expenditure and we get a cost of 10½d. per bush per year for a wonderful display of bloom and very little work. When weighing up the merits of herbaceous borders (which no one bothers to cost), bedding plants and, more particularly, shrubs, it is well worthwhile to keep this rose budget in mind.

COST OF GARDEN DESCRIBED IN CHAPTER XIII

The cost of the small (Sister Ann) rose and shrub garden described and illustrated in Chapter XIII was (in 1961):

	£	s.	d.
Western Red Cedar timber (including delivery)	22	5	0
1,500 Bricks, seconds (including delivery)	18	15	0
Ballast, sand, cement and nails	7	10	0
64 hours' direct labour (week-end)	16	0	0
Plants (including delivery):			
24 Cotoneaster franchetii	8	10	0
5 Viburnum davidii	2	15	0
5 Caryopteris clandonensis	2	0	0
200 Dutch dwarf lavender (pot seedlings)	8	10	0
24 Bearded iris	6	10	0
12 Allwoodii pinks	2	2	0
3 Clematis montana grandiflora	1	10	0
2 Clematis Gipsy Queen	1	10	0
12 Pillar roses at 72s. a doz.	3	12	0
18 Shrub roses at 72s. a doz.	5	8	0
96 Bush roses at 55s. a doz.	22	0	0
Western Red Cedar Seat	8	10	0
Sculpture (by author)			Nil
Total	£137	7	0

But do not let us end on the sordid note of money; rather should we remember the sagacity of William Paul when he said — so long ago and still so true — 'the popularity of the rose rests on a sure foundation — its intrinsic merit — what other genus of plant embraces so great a variety of character, or gives forth such a number of delicious blossoms for so long a period? Moreover, it is easy of culture; suited to a great variety of soils, lives and blooms even when neglected; yet yields an abundant return for whatever labour may be bestowed upon it'.

Remember too that our rose growing should be a relaxation, not a burden. Naturally one tries to grow them well, but good blooms or not so good blooms they are, like other things in the garden, the product of one's care and effort and they will be precious on that account alone. It was written of Sergeant Cuff when he had retired, that 'he was living out the Sybarite years of his life smothered in roses'. How happy he must have been — greenfly, black spot and all.

RECOMMENDED READING

Successful Rose Growing. A. NORMAN. (W. H. & L. Collingridge Ltd)
    for its practical detail and commonsense in all aspects of rose
    growing.
The Rose In Britain. N. P. HARVEY. (Souvenir Press Ltd)
    for its chapter on fragrance and its individual assessment of varieties.
Collins Guide to Roses. BERTRAM PARK.
    for its comprehensiveness in all fields.
Roses. F. FAIRBROTHER. (Penguin Handbook)
    for its chapter on the History of the Rose and for *multum in parvo*.
The Old Shrub Roses. G. S. THOMAS. (Phoenix House).
The Literature of The National Rose Society (St Albans, Herts.)

Index

The figures in bold type indicate main references: those in parentheses refer to the line drawings in the text.

181